William Kingsford

**The Early Bibliography of the Province of Ontario**

Dominion of Canada, with other Information

William Kingsford

**The Early Bibliography of the Province of Ontario**
*Dominion of Canada, with other Information*

ISBN/EAN: 9783337205591

Printed in Europe, USA, Canada, Australia, Japan

Cover: Foto ©ninafisch / pixelio.de

More available books at **www.hansebooks.com**

THE

# EARLY BIBLIOGRAPHY

OF THE

## PROVINCE OF ONTARIO,

DOMINION OF CANADA,

WITH OTHER INFORMATION.

A SUPPLEMENTAL CHAPTER OF CANADIAN ARCHÆOLOGY.

BY

WILLIAM KINGSFORD, LL.D., F.R.S. [C.]

TORONTO:
ROWSELL & HUTCHISON.
MONTREAL:
EBEN PICKEN.
1892.

"Every work must be judged by its design, and is to be valued by its result."

DISRAELI, "Curiosities of Literature."
Preface, 1839.

———

"Ich weiss wohl," sagte Goethe, "dass es schwer ist, aber die Auffassung und Darstellung des Besondern ist auch das eigentliche Leben der Kunst." Mitwoch den 29 October, 1823.
Gespräche mit Goethe in den letzen Jahren seines Lebens.

JOHANN PETER ECKERMAN.

["I know well it is hard," said Goethe, "but the apprehension and representation of what is special is also the real life of art."]
Wednesday, the 29th of October, 1823.
Conversations with Goethe in the last years of his life.

JOHN PETER ECKERMAN.

# EARLY BIBLIOGRAPHY.

Six years ago, in 1886, I published a work on Canadian Archæology, in which I endeavoured to give a history of the first printed books in the provinces of Quebec and Ontario. There was no great difficulty with regard to the former. The subject had been closely studied for some years by men of acknowledged attainments; and, although not reduced to form and system, and somewhat scattered, much valuable information had been gathered. I was particularly indebted to my accomplished friend, Abbé Verreault, who threw open to me the wealth of his library and the hospitality of his home, the first of the many occasions which I have passed in his society and of the men gathered about him. I may mention especially the late Sheriff Chauveau, whom I constantly met there, and Mr. Desmazures, a Saint Sulpician of rare learning. In Ottawa, Mr. de Celles, of the Library, aided me with his knowledge, and I was thus enabled to bring together, in an accessible form, what information had been obtained about the early literary history of the province of Quebec. It is conceded by all whose opinions are in any way worthy of respect that the printing-press was unknown in the French regime, and that the history of printing books dates from the conquest. I have entered into this subject at length in the volume in question; therefore, there is no need for reference to it in this place. What is there related, gathered from the knowledge of those who preceded me, is admitted to be correct; at least, I have not heard that any part of the narrative has been impugned.

I did not experience the same good fortune in Ontario. The subject, I will venture the remark, had never received even slight attention until I approached it, and consequently my endeavour to obtain reliable information was not attended with success. Those to whom I addressed myself, who I regarded as having knowledge concerning the bibliography of Ontario, had not considered it from the aspect submitted by me; and although there was every desire to assist me, I found few who were capable of doing so. Dr. Brymner gave me whatever aid he was able, and Mr. Beverley Robinson, then Lieutenant-Governor of Ontario, made great exertions to learn the titles of the first printed books. Mr. Robinson had during his government rendered excellent service in a cognate branch of inquiry. With great labour on his part he was enabled to obtain access to the original portraits of the governors and the administrators of the former province of Upper Canada, from its first establishment: and the liberality of the Legislature enabled him to obtain copies of what may be unhesitatingly pronounced to be authentic portraits of the governors to the union of the province; except in the case of Governor Peter Hunter, of whom no portrait can be found. It is to me astounding that so little recognition has been made of the labours of Mr. Beverley Robinson, and also of his brother, Colonel Robinson, of the imperial service, in thus bringing together this valuable collection which the province possesses. Few even know of the existence of these portraits; certainly few have borne testimony to the labour and perseverance with which Mr.

Robinson followed out his plan until he had perfected the collection to the fullest extent possible. It exacted a long and often embarrassing correspondence with the family in whose possession the portrait was to be found. Access to it had to be obtained, and copies made to be sent to Canada. Ontario is singularly fortunate in possessing, in a connected series, portraits of her governors from the earliest date : not fanciful works of art, christened by auctioneers and dealers, but of undoubted authenticity.

An acknowledgment must also be made to Sir Oliver Mowat and the members of his Government, for their ready acceptance of Mr. Beverley Robinson's proposition, and for obtaining from the Legislature the material aid to carry it out. It is a passage in Ontario political life of pleasant memory, and reflects honour on the Legislature of that period, and on all concerned.

The inquiries, which at the time were continued with some pertinacity, ended in the conclusion that the first Ontario book, "out of the domain of Statute Law and the Parliamentary Journals," was printed in the year 1832 ; when the History of the War of 1812, by David Thompson, "Printed by T. Sewell, Printer, Book-binder and Stationer, Market Square, Niagara, 1832," was published. The statement remained uncontradicted until 1888, when public attention was drawn to the subject, and Mr. Gagnon, of Saint Roch, Quebec, in a published letter gave the names of several earlier volumes, some of which are in his possession, and he established by catalogues that other works were known. A correspondence on this point took place in the Toronto *Mail*, and some discussion was awakened. Since that date Mr. Gagnon has continued his research, and Mr. Bain, of the Toronto Library, has likewise made great exertions to increase our knowledge on the subject.

As much has been learned since the publication of my former volume, which, I will take upon myself to say, gave the first impetus to this inquiry, I consider that the time has arrived when a supplementary chapter can be profitably written, embodying the information which has been obtained. I have accordingly methodized, in the form now presented, the facts we now possess. I by no means claim them to be final. I trust, however, within the limit enforced upon me, they will be found in the words of Juvenal to be

         . . . remota

Erroris nebula . . .

Whatever the imperfections of the list now published, it is certainly far in advance of the conclusions expressed in the work of 1886. I have to acknowledge the courtesy of those friends who aided me in this inquiry, to whom I feel under great obligation for communicating many of the leading facts.

In my former work, I excepted publications bearing upon statute law, journals of the legislature and pamphlets. I purpose in this compilation to include every description of printed book which will throw light on the social condition of this early period. I cannot claim the record to be beyond dispute. It is scarcely possible to attain this result even with a far greater extent of labour and inquiry than I am able to devote to the subject. I trust, however, that I will be enabled clearly to establish the continued progress made in our political life, and to furnish my testimony to the increased literary activity observable from the days of the first lieutenant-governor.

At the time of the passage of the Canada Act, on the 14th of March, 1791, constituting the two distinct provinces of Upper and Lower Canada, Lord Dorchester was governor-in-chief. He had held that position since 1786, having been named in succession to Haldimand. The latter left Canada in 1784, the Government having been administered in the intervening two years by Hamilton, and afterwards by Hope. Dorchester remained in Canada until the 18th of August, 1791, when Sir Alured Clarke was sworn in as lieutenant-governor and commander-in-chief. On the 17th of November of this year, Simcoe arrived at Quebec, bringing with him instructions restricting Clarke's powers to Lower Canada, with an official copy of the new act and instructions to divide the province of Quebec into the newly-established political divisions of Upper and Lower Canada. The proclamation was accordingly issued declaring the division, which took effect on the 26th of December, 1791. Simcoe remained the winter at Quebec, and it was not until the summer of 1792 he reached Upper Canada. On the 16th of July he issued a proclamation, in which he established the electoral divisions for which representatives should be returned.

The members chosen for these electoral districts forming the first legislature of Upper Canada met at Newark [Niagara] on Monday, the 17th of September, 1792. According- ing to the official reports of that meeting, it was on that day that Simcoe made his opening speech, which inaugurated the working of the constitution in Upper Canada. A copy of this speech, with the replies of the Legislative Council and of the House of Assembly, with Simcoe's speech on the prorogation of Wednesday, the 15th of October, has been preserved. I have not heard of there being a second copy. If this sheet be genuine, it is the earliest example of political printing in Ontario. But doubts have been strongly ex- pressed on this point by those capable of judging; and it has been supposed that the sheet in question is a reprint of a later date; at what time it cannot even be surmised.

There is an extraordinary mistake in this paper. The official copy of the proceedings of the House unmistakably establish that Simcoe's speech was delivered on Monday, the 17th of September, whereas the date given in this sheet is Tuesday, the 18th of September. No printer's name is attached. By a strange coincidence, Gourlay, when alluding to this speech, mentions the date of its delivery similarly to that as it appears on the sheet, and the printed italic lines are identical in the two. Arguing that we are dealing with a reprint, the query is pertinent: Did Gourlay follow the reprint, or the reprint Gourlay? Moreover, the type of the sheet has been pronounced as not being that of a font in use in Niagara at the time.

There is a minor fact in connection with this proceeding. On the 29th of November, 1792, Simcoe transmits to King, the Under-Secretary of State, an "authentic" copy of the speech delivered at the prorogation on the 15th of October, 1792. [Can. Arch., Q. 279, I., p. 217.] The letter consists of only a few lines, and explains that this course has been taken owing to the first copy sent having been inaccurate. The sheet itself is undoubtedly official in character: it is not an utter impossibility that it was printed to be included in Simcoe's letter of the 29th of November. No occasion suggests itself why a reprint should have been made at any time. The error of date which escaped observation could have crept in at an early, as at a later period. The same remark is applicable to the introduction of italics. It is likewise worthy of notice that only one copy of this paper is known, and that its pedigree is traceable to the descendants of Mr. Powell, subsequently Clerk of the House. I do not feel myself called upon to do more than to state the facts as I have heard them narrated. I venture, however, to express the opinion, that it could not be a reprint from Gourlay, because that volume* gives only the speeches of Simcoe on opening and proroguing the legislature, and not the address in answer to the speech, either of the legislative council, or of the house of assembly; whereas, both are reported in the paper in question.

The authenticity of this sheet to some extent includes the inquiry whether at this date a printing press was in operation at Newark. Louis Roy was the printer of the first paper in Ontario, "*The Upper Canada Gazette* or *American Oracle*," which appeared on the 13th of April, 1793. This paper continued to be printed at Niagara until August, 1798. It appeared in York [Toronto] the following October. Whether Roy's undertaking was the result of his own enterprise, or was commenced through the intervention of Simcoe, it is not easy positively to determine. It is not unreasonable to suppose that to some extent it owed its origin to Simcoe, who had passed the preceding winter at Quebec. On the 16th of July, 1792, Simcoe issued his proclamation dividing the province into electoral districts, which, doubtless, was printed, and has been preserved to posterity by having been included in the statutes of 1831, of Hugh C. Thompson and James Macfarlane. The belief has been expressed that the document was prepared at Quebec previous to Simcoe's ascent of the Saint Lawrence; and it is a reasonable supposition that Simcoe furnished sufficient inducements for a printer to establish himself at the new seat of government, when, as Governor, he entered upon his duties. In judging the genuineness of the sheet in question, it must also be borne in mind that it was printed, if contemporary, six months previous to the establishment of Roy's paper; a fact

---

* "Statistical Account of Upper Canada, compiled with a View to a Grand System of Emigration."
Robert Gourlay. London, 1822. Vol. II. p. 110.

which may explain the difference of type that has been
pointed out.*

Very little is known of the early journals of the House of
Assembly, and the opinion prevails that they were not
regularly printed until 1820 or 1821. The first printed copy
in the Parliamentary Library is that of the session of 1821.
The publication of the journals of the House, so far as is
known, did not take place until 1801, when £300 [$1200]
was granted for printing the acts and journals [1st Session,
3rd Parliament].

The title of this volume was :—

"Journal | of the | House of Assembly | of    Upper
Canada ' From the twenty-eighth of May to the ninth of
July, 1801 | both days inclusive | In the forty-first year of
the reign of | King George the Third | Being the first Session
of the Third Provincial Parliament of this | Province | York,

---

* In Sabin's " Bibliothera Americana," Vol. XIX., p. 568, the
following notice is taken of Simcoe's speech :—
" SIMCOE.    Speech of John Graves Simcoe, Esq.    *    *    Nigara
[sic].    Printed 1796.    Svo.    Also, Speech    *    *    Printed in Upper
Canada by Louis Roy, 1793.    Svo.    These two titles are taken from
a bookseller's catalogue."

Roy did not remain more than some months in Upper Canada.
The first number of the Upper Canada Gazette, printed by him in
Niagara, appeared on the 18th April, 1793.    There is ground for
the opinion that he took part in the establishment of the Montreal
Gazette, the first number of which was published on the 3rd of
August, 1795.    It is not known when Roy left Niagara.

One of the earliest examples of political printing is in the possession of Mr. Bain, Toronto : " Proclamation on the Settlement of
Lands."    Reprinted at Newark by " G. Tiffany, 1795."

Upper Canada : Printed by order of the House of Assembly, by John Bennett | Printer to the King's most excellent Majesty | 1801." 4to. pp. viii., and 66pp.

If the journals of 1802 and 1803 were printed, no copies are extant. In the 4th Session, 1804, the Act was repealed, £80 out of the £300 being appropriated for the statutes. In 1806, the proceedings in the second Session of the 4th Parliament were published, in 8vo, 34pp.

I believe it may be assumed that the journals were printed until 1806. After that year they were discontinued, owing to the expense ; such being the cause assigned in a despatch of Lieutenant-Governor Gore to the Honourable William Windham. They were certainly printed in 1821, whether previously to that date cannot be stated. The impression, however, prevails that the printed journals were only resumed at that date. No copies are known for the years 1822, 1823 and 1824, after which time they are regularly continued.

The above account may not be considered very satisfactory, but it is all that is known. Mr. Bain, of the Toronto Library, who has bestowed much careful consideration to the subject, may be regarded as an authority for the knowledge we possess. I have to acknowledge his valuable assistance in the compilation I have made. I may thus claim to have gathered all the information obtainable ; it must remain in its present condition, until supplemented by others who are better informed.

Thus it may be said there are no printed copies of the journals of the Legislature of the old province of Upper Canada to be found previous to 1825. The few scattered odd numbers which remain are in the hands of book collectors. The journals themselves are in MS. in the Parliamentary Library, having been obtained from the

Colonial Office. Some years, however, are absent, but they are to be found elsewhere in the Dominion.

This is hardly the condition in which we should find the journals of the first parliaments of the wealthy province of Ontario. I venture, therefore, to bring the subject to the attention of Sir Oliver Mowat and his ministry, so that they can consider the wisdom of having them copied and printed. Sir Oliver Mowat, himself a man of letters, will not, I am sure, fail to see the force of this recommendation. His government has always acted as the patron of literature and art in striking and honourable contrast to the Dominion government, which pertinaciously frowns down and discourages all literary labour, except that of the enforced duty of assuring their continuance in power.

"See the players well bestowed" says Hamlet to Polonius. "Do you hear, let them be well used, for they are the abstract and brief chronicles of the time : after your death you were better have a bad epitaph than ill report while you live." Those who turn the deaf ear of ignorant indifference to the claims of honest literature would do well to ponder over these words. It is a time when false reputations are on one side swept away, on the other when merit obtains sure, if slow, recognition. It is an age of intelligence to call forth a nemesis for all neglect of duty ; and however great the temporary success conferred by power, the hour is certain, early or late, when every prominent career will be fairly judged. Those who have lived on purchased praise will hereafter take their true place in history, be it good or bad, according to their deserts.

Sir Oliver Mowat* has shewn broad and generous views in

---

* The honour which Sir Oliver Mowat received from the hand of the Queen on the observance of her last birthday, has led to some strange comment. In my poor judgment, the acceptance

his recognition of the claims of literature and art. His support of Mr. Beverley Robinson in his endeavour to bring together the valuable gallery of the portraits of the governors of Ontario, can never be forgotten, for the portraits will remain for all time.

In the humble view of the writer, these journals should be copied and printed. They would not make above four volumes of 500 pp., and the cost would not exceed some sum between $4,000 to $6,000. There is no necessity for a large edition; five hundred copies would be sufficient for the legislature and the public libraries, with a certain number offered for private sale at the cost of paper and printing.

It requires no argument to sustain the view that the documentary history of the country is incomplete until these journals are made accessible. There is much which can still be learned from them. They form the early record of our first political being, and to the student there is much that may be read with profit.

It is not on the ground of obtaining symmetry in the list of public documents available to research, that this course is advocated, but from the feeling of the public utility which will be derived by its adoption.

---

of such a distinction is purely a matter which concerns the recipient alone. It is for him to determine whether his circumstances, his antecedents, his sentiments, justify its acceptance. The *doctrinaire* opinion, which ignores this feeling, is, as Pope tells us, " but leather or prunella. Those who, with myself, sympathise with Sir Oliver's devotion to the great British Empire, and remember his useful and honourable life, have given him their warmest unconditional congratulations, with the hope he will long live to enjoy the distinction. It will be the historian's duty to record of him : " he did love his country ; it honoured him."

There is ground for belief that the Statutes were regularly printed year by year from 1792, although but few of the early statutes are in existence. The only yearly volumes known to be preserved are in the Toronto Library, viz., 1798, 1799, 1800, 1801. The fact of the early annual publication is established by the following advertisement, which appears in the *Upper Canada Gazette*, Vol. III., No. 3, 9th November, 1796 :—"Just received and ready to be delivered, 'The Laws of the 5th Session,' with a table of contents to the whole volumes complete." The first consolidation of the statutes, according to the title page, was made in 1802. It is a question if the date was a misprint, for the volume includes the Acts of the Sessions of 1803–1804. It is probable that the later statutes may have been subsequently published as a continuation of the volume, and issued as a supplement. The volume is a small 4to. The title :—

"The | Statutes | of His Majesty's Province of ' Upper Canada | enacted by the King's Most Excellent Majesty by and with the consent of the | Legislative Council and Assembly of the said Province, constituted and assembled by virtue | of and under the authority of an Act of Parliament of Great Britain, &c., &c., York | Printed under the authority and by command of His Excellency Peter ; Hunter, Esquire, Lieutenant Governor of the Province of Upper Canada, and Lieutenant General commanding His Majesty's forces in Upper and Lower | Canada, By John Bennett, Printer to the King's Most Excellent Majesty | 1802."

The Upper Canadian Acts are preceded by several Imperial Acts. An index closes the volume. Mr. Bain, to whom I am indebted for this information, points out that throughout the heading of the volume the "Fourth Session of the Fourth Parliament" is printed instead of "Third Parliament." A correction of this mistake is made in the "Errata."

A second consolidation was made in 1811, published at "York, Upper Canada." Printed by John Cameron . . . 1811. A large 4to.

The third consolidation was carried out in 1818 : "The | Provincial statutes of | Upper Canada | revised corrected and republished | by | authority | Samuel Smith Esquire administrator | York printed by R. C. Horne 1818." Small 4to.

This volume, although bearing the date 1818, contains the statutes of 1819.

A complete edition of the statutes compiled by Nickalls was published at Kingston in 1831, containing all public acts from 1791 to 1831.

In 1843 an edition was published at Toronto by Stanton, which contained all the acts passed by the Upper Canada Legislature. It consisted of two volumes : Vol. I., the public acts from 1792 to 1840; Vol. II., the local and private acts from 1822 to 1839.

In 1794 an advertisement appeared in the *Upper Canada Gazette* announcing the publication of an almanac for 1795. No copy is known.

It is a question if it ever appeared. The fact is suggested by the publication of the following advertisement in the same paper, Vol. III., No. 6. 30th November, 1796 : "Now preparing, and in a few days will be committed to

B

the press, 'The Upper Canada Calendar for the year 1797, being a Pocket Almanack, containing, besides astronomical calculations, lists of the Legislative, Executive and Military Officers, times and places of holding Courts, etc. *Being the first work of the kind ev-r attempted in this province. (sic.)* The publisher most respectfully solicits the assistance of every gentleman who possesses the means of promoting the design, by furnishing him with articles properly arranged (and) such particulars as may be in their power."

No copy of this almanac has come down to us, and the number of years it was continued is, likewise, a matter of uncertainty.

It is a curious fact, considering the small population of Upper Canada at that time, that there should have been rival almanacs for the year 1802. One was published at Niagara, by Tiffany, one at York, by Bennett. The former is thus advertised, in its way a curiosity :—

"Tiffany's Upper Canada Almanack for the year 1802, and from the creation, according to the Scriptures, 5764. Being the sixth after bissextile, or leap year, calculated for the meridian of Niagara, etc. Niagara : Published by Sylvester Tiffany, and sold by him at the *Herald* office, by the merchants in town, also at York, Kingston, Detroit, Queenstown, Chippewa, and Fort Erie. Said Tiffany publishes every Saturday a newspaper entitled the *Herald.* Subscriptions are received for it in all the principal towns of the province."

Two copies of this publication have been preserved, one in the possession of Mr. Gagnon, of Quebec, one belonging to Mr. Bain.

This almanac furnishes the names of the officials, with a list of the Sessions of the Law Courts. We may there read some somewhat tame anecdotes with several receipts, such as how to preserve fruit, to pickle cabbage, to make currant wine, etc. Its *cheval de bataille,* however, was, that it was a weather almanac, and offered, in the most approved fashion, the advice weather-prophets give in modern times : "clear and pleasant," "now look out for a storm," "snow," "a few days of blustering weather, look well to your cattle," "fine growing weather," "look out for a long wet season," "thunder and rain," and so on. The writer, however, does not plead infallibility, and asks for forgiveness if the information prove "erroneous," and that "careful observers" will "throw over the error the excess of that charity of which their generous souls are composed."

There is another effort on the part of the compiler; he undertakes to warn his readers against the diseases incident to humanity, by the passage of the moon in the heavens. To this day we find on the covers of many advertising almanacs of quack medicines, the figure of a man erect, the different parts of whose body are referred to the signs of the Zodiac. A belief in astrology continues to identify the moon's path as threatening humanity with diseases in certain directions; thus, when the moon is in *Aries* there is always danger of convulsions, bad eyes, weak knees, etc.* In the almanac

---

* DISEASES OF THE MOON.

Moon in *Aries* signifies convulsions, defluxions of rheum from the head, lethargy, weakness in the eyes and pains in the knees.

Moon in *Taurus* produces pains in the legs and feet, swellings, stoppage, sore throat, etc.

Moon in *Gemini* denotes a wandering gout in the legs, arms, hands and feet ; surfeits and great obstructions.

Moon in *Cancer* shews the stomach much afflicted, a surfeit, small-pox, convulsions, falling sickness, tympany, or dropsy.

Moon in *Leo*, the heart afflicted, sore throat, quinsy, king's evil, etc.

Moon in *Virgo* signifies great pain and disorders in the bowels, melancholy blood, obstructions, weakness in the arms and shoulders.

the passage of the moon is not set forth by the signs of the Zodiac, but by the parts of the human frame liable to suffer at certain periods from lunar influence. The use of this phraseology conveys the opinion that belief in astrology then prevailed, and that the language was fitted for a market ready to accept it.

I am sorry to say that I have been unable to obtain reference to the Upper Canada Almanac of 1802, of Bennett, the Government Printer, at York [Toronto]. A copy, however, is known to be in existence.

In 1823 Mr. Fothergill commenced the publication of a York Almanac and Royal Calendar of Upper Canada, 12mo., 160 pp., which was continued during 1824, 1825, 1826, increasing its size to 196pp., containing likewise an additional 100pp. of chronological detail, independently numbered, suggesting that it was a distinct publication and sold separately.

I have alluded (Archæology, p. 77) to Mr. Fothergill's

---

Moon in *Libra* denotes the reins are distempered, obstructions in the stomach, weakness in the back, whites in women, surfeits, pleurisy, etc.

Moon in *Scorpio* shews the distemper is in the secrets, small-pox, dropsy, poison, the heart afflicted, swoonings, etc.

Moon in *Sagittarius* imports lameness or weakness in the thighs, distempers in the bowels, etc.

Moon in *Capricorn* signifies the stone, weak back, gout in the knees, whites in women, etc.

Moon in *Aquarius* signifies hysterics, swellings and pains in the legs and secret parts.

Moon in *Pisces* shews cold taken in the feet and body disordered thereby; swellings in the legs, dropsies, and the body overcharged with moist humours.

[Grammar of Astrology, containing all things necessary calculating a nativity * * * by Zadkiel. *Dedicated to the University of Cambridge!* London, 1849 [pp. 177-8.]

dismissal from his position as Queen's Printer in 1825 by Sir Peregrine Maitland. As a member of the House, Mr. Fothergill had claimed that information concerning the post-office revenue should be submitted. He had otherwise shewn some liberal views, a proceeding on his part which suggested to the authorities he was an unfit person to hold any public office.

The almanac of Mr. Lyon Mackenzie first appeared in 1830. No. II. remains preserved ; its title is " Poor Richard, or the Yorkshire Almanack for the Year of our Lord 1831." By Patrick Swift, York. Printed at the office of the *Colonial Advocate* by William Lyon Mackenzie ; pp. 16, 8vo.

There is no precise knowledge of the number of almanacs published by Mr. Lyon Mackenzie. By general consent 1834 is considered to be the latest date : on this theory five were issued [1830–1834]. I have been unable to refer to the copy mentioned by me.

I have given in the volume of 1886 the history of the establishment of the Archive office. The collection of original documents, since this date, has been continued with regularity and with remarkable energy. In the twenty years which have elapsed since its foundation, the issue of the annual reports has been uninterrupted. They contain the authenticated narrative of events which, it may safely be said, will much modify, and in many cases, will entirely change the published opinions that have hitherto passed for history. Nowhere are these reports more sought for than in the United States. There is not a library, or an historical society worthy the name in the republic, which does not possess them. There is no historical writer of reputation who hesitates to accept them as authority. Dr. Brynner's industry has been remarkable, and it is best known to those who have been busied in these investigations. The sustained power apparent in these reports year after year has added to the reputation of the province with those who believe that there is something higher in life than material success and mere temporary political notoriety.

The first report appeared in 1872 by Dr. Brynner.
" second "       "       " 1873 "       "
" third       "       "       " 1874 by Abbé Verreault.

The Abbé at this date was deputed to make examinations, in the first place in London, afterwards at Lille, Liège and Metz, finally at Paris. The three above named reports are included in the general reports of the Minister of Agriculture and must there be sought for.

The succeeding five years were passed in classifying, arranging and calendaring to some extent the records and documents which form the wealth of the department, and generally in systematizing for reference the books and papers. I must refer my reader to the description of the department made by me in my previous volume. The series of independent reports commenced in 1881. The first of this issue was confined to a specification of what had then been obtained and methodized. In 1882 some returns of 1791 were published concerning shipping and exports and imports. In 1883 the publication of original documents was commenced. In 1884 the calendar of the Haldimand collection first appeared, which papers, including the Bouquet papers and the Haldimand diary, were continued until 1889, inclusive. This calendar, which is unusually full, alone fills three large volumes. During the last two years the calendar of the State papers since the conquest, affecting British Canada, has been commenced; those of Upper Canada having been begun in the report of 1891.

Even so far as these publications extend, they furnish several important volumes of acknowledged value.

There can be little doubt with regard to the benefit conferred on the study of the history of the continent by the establishment of the archive branch. If truth is to be the guiding principle in any narrative, access to the documentary evidence affecting it is indispensable. Until the carefully-made transcripts of the imperial record office were open to investigation in Ottawa, they might be regarded as so many sealed volumes; such was the difficulty of obtaining access to them. The fact may be recognized in the number of investigators from the United States, who have patiently examined these papers, with a view of penetrating to the sources of events bearing upon the different periods they were studying. A multiplied amount of data can be found referring to the northern states of the Union, extending from the seaboard to the Mississippi. The consequence has been that the office has in the United States acquired a good name for its value and usefulness, which forms the highest tribute to the wisdom of its establishment.

The several MS. volumes of transcripts from imperial documents may be briefly described.

The Bouquet papers of 34 volumes. Bouquet's services in the Indian wars of 1763 are now commencing to be better known and appreciated.

The Haldimand papers of 232 volumes. Haldimand was governor of Canada from 1778 to 1784; a born collector, he has retained for us much information which otherwise would entirely have passed away.

Many volumes of State papers [1755–1760] including the military correspondence.

The State papers bearing upon the new Province of Canada continued to the Canada Act in 1791. After that date there is a division between those of Upper and Lower Canada; accordingly, they form two distinct series, and are in process of being so calendared. According to the report of 1891, those of Lower Canada have been calendared to 1800; those of Upper Canada to 1801.

Many volumes of military correspondence are open to reference. They were originally collected in Canada with the design of being transmitted to the Home War Office. They have, however, been permitted to be retained in Canada. This important collection, which covers a period of nearly ninety years, consists of a large number of volumes. All are indexed, so reference to any subject can be immediate.

In addition to the above described MS. volumes, a staff of copyists is at present engaged in Paris making selected extracts from the records, commencing from the middle of the seventeenth century : several volumes of these excerpts have been received.

There is a series consisting of several volumes of warrants, shewing the amounts paid to officials and others, with the vouchers of the various payments made by the Lake-Marine and other departments from 1784 to about 1811.

Independently of this official correspondence, the branch possesses an extensive collection of family papers, in several instances of those who in their lives were persons of prominence, containing important official and private correspondence. These letters throw much light on contemporary events, and often explain the secret working of much, otherwise difficult to be understood. They are of great value to the writer of history, and cannot fail to be consulted by every student. They are perfectly arranged, so that they are in every respect accessible, and are thus of essential service to any one investigating the period to which they relate.

In connection with these MS. volumes, there is a large collection of printed books bearing upon the history of the dominion. They consist of the official volumes issued by the mother country and the several states of the Union. The history of Canada, and of all the Northern States to the Mississippi, is so much interwoven as on many points to be almost one and the same; consequently, the documents enumerated by me are of equally recognized importance without the province. Access can also be had to the collection of published volumes which appeared at the time, or immediately after the events narrated. It is true that they are not all gospel: many are the production of passionate sentiment in one or the other direction; many are stamped by what Jean Baptiste Biot* called that "geographical selfishness, patriotism"; many uncertain in their information; many hard reading.

But with all their faults no historical library can be held to be complete without them. It is of great importance that these volumes should be accessible at the time when the MSS. are being consulted. Possible reference to them by the skilled investigator, engaged in the study of the original calendared documents, is of immense value. They go very far to aid what should be the first duty of every

* The eminent French natural philosopher, whose researches as to the polarization of light in 1840 gained for him the Rumford medal of the Royal Society.

man in his private life equally with his duty as a public writer ; the establishment of truth.

Dr. Brymner has paid particular attention to the collection of pamphlets,* the collection consisting of very many volumes of considerable value.

I do not think it an exaggeration when I add that the establishment of the Canadian Archive office in Ottawa has given a strong impetus to historical studies throughout the whole continent, extending to the gulf of Mexico and west of the Mississippi. Historical societies not previously existent have been established, and those which were hitherto the most active have received an increased impulse to their usefulness. There is one point on which I may dwell : the perfect fidelity with which all the original documents of the Canadian Archive office are transcribed, and the strict adherence to the text. On the other hand, contemporary printed books, however adverse to the good name of Canada

---

* The despised pamphlet has of late years risen somewhat in estimation. Everyone who has commercially had the misfortune to publish a pamphlet knows by experience that they never sell : they prove an invariable loss to the writer. But they have this advantage, they relate an event in its true character ; and however painful of remembrance to the contemptible perpetrator of a wrong, it is a record out of which, whatever his cunning and falsehood, he cannot writhe or wriggle. The State Historical Society of Wisconsin, which has collected 150,000 volumes, in a late appeal for continued aid, thus remarks on the importance of contributing pamphlets of every kind :— " Ephemeral in form of publication and commonly thought not worthy of preservation, pamphlets are often difficult to collect a short time after issue. They reflect the spirit and sentiments of the age, however, better than elaborate treatises and are indispensable treasures in a good reference library, where historians, biographers, statisticians and men of letters in general, naturally look for everything, no matter how apparently trivial, that may shed light on the subjects of their investigation."

and its institutions, are kept for reference, to shew the difference of view in that, and other respects.

I will venture to speak of a requirement, generally admitted: the necessity of a proper fire-proof building where these costly documents should be preserved, and, at the same time, the requirements of historical students be considered. Many of these gentlemen come from the United States. Any national pride we may feel in the fact that the Archives are sought for reference by the public writers of the republic, is certainly not heightened by seeing them engaged in the small and not too convenient room where their labours have to be conducted, and where, when more than three or four are gathered together, one is reminded of the narrative of the pursuit of knowledge under difficulties. Perhaps some day we may again meet in the executive a reawakening of the feeling that led to the establishment of the institution, and which may dictate the construction of a proper building, efficiently adapted to its uses in all respects.

For the present, however, we can only say with Cicero, "*speremus quæ volumus*"; adding what his philosophy also teaches us, "*sed quæ acciderint feramus.*" *

The first printed pamphlet in Ontario, so far as is known, appeared during the war of 1812–14.

1. [1814]. "A Form of Prayer and Thanksgiving to Almighty God to be used on Friday, the Third Day of June, 1814, being the day appointed by Proclamation for a General Thanksgiving to Almighty God, To acknowledge the great Goodness and Mercy of Almighty God, who in addition to the manifold and inestimable Benefits which we have received at His Hands has continued to us His Pro-

---

* Let us hope for that which we desire, but let us bear what falls to our lot.

tection and Assistance in the War in which we are now
engaged, and has given to the Arms of His Majesty and to
those of His Allies a Series of Signal and Glorious Victories
over the Forces of the Enemy." Kingston. Printed by
Stephen Miles ; pp. 14., 12o. 1814.

One of the earliest books printed in the province of
Ontario is a pamphlet known by an advertisement in the
*Quebec Gazette* of the 12th of November, 1818. It is
believed that no copy of it can be found. The author was
Robert Gourlay, to whose unfortunate career I have alluded in
"Canadian Archæology" [pp. 84–85]. The treatment which
Gourlay received is a painful passage in Upper Canadian
history.

2. [1818]. For sale at this office, price 1s. "Principles
and proceedings of the inhabitants of the District of Niagara
for addressing His Royal Highness the Prince Regent,
respecting claims of sufferers in the late War, Lands to
Militia men, and the general benefit of Upper Canada.
Printed at the *Niagara Spectator* Office, 1818."

3. [1818]. "Proceedings at a meeting of the inhabitants
of the Townships of Hope and Hamilton, in the district of
Newcastle, U.C., held agreeable to notice from Robert
Gourlay." York, U.C. Printed by R. C. Horne. 1818.

A copy of this extremely rare work is in the Toronto
Library ; from what I learn, it may be considered to be
*unique.*

The following books were published at the dates named:—

4. [1822]. "An | Address | to the | liege men | of
every British Colony | and | province | in the world | by
a friend to his species. Kingston : | Printed at the *Herald*
Office, | 1822." 12mo.

This pamphlet is in verse, and consists of 13pp. It is in
the possession of Mr. Gagnon.

Mr. Edward Allen Talbot, in his work, "Five years residence in Canada," London, 1824, Vol. II., p. 192, makes mention of the following work. I cannot learn that a copy has been preserved : it, however, forms the second part of the almanac for 1822.

5. [1822]. "A Sketch of the present state of Canada. York, Upper Canada, 1822." By Mr. Fothergill.

I have previously alluded to this gentleman's removal, in 1825, from the office of Queen's printer, which he held.

6. [1822]. "Sermon and Catechism for Children." York. Printed by J. Carey, 1822 ; pp. 16., 12mo.

7. [1823]. "Constitution of the Antient Fraternity of Free and Accepted Masons. Part the second, containing the charges, regulations, etc. Published by the authority of the United Grand Lodge, by William Williams, Esq. First Canadian edition. Republished by order of the Provincial Grand Lodge of Upper Canada. Kingston, 1823." 8vo. 96pp.

This title is taken from the catalogue of Haight & Co., No. 1, 1890.

8. "St. Ursula's Convent, or the Nun of Canada, containing scenes of Real Life, Kingston, Upper Canada, 1824." I cannot learn that a copy is in existence. The book is known by allusion to it in the *Canadian Review and Literary and Historical Journal,* in which it is reviewed at some length in the first number in July, 1824, and it is by no means favourably noticed.

This *Canadian Review* was edited by Dr. A. J. Christie, grandfather of Mr. A. J. Christie, Q.C., Ottawa. He came to this country in 1818, one of three sons of the non-juror Episcopal rector of the parish of Woodhead, near Fyvie, Aberdeenshire. He was for some time editor of the Montreal *Gazette* and *Herald,* following the medical profession at the same time. His son, Mr. Thomas A. Christie, started the Bytown *Gazette* in 1836. The *Canadian Review* was brought out irregularly in 1824 and 1826. Of the five numbers I have seen, the first three were printed at the office of the Montreal *Herald*, the last two at the office of the Montreal *Gazette*. All the articles are characterized by literary power, as the work of well educated and able men. The tone of them is admirable.

The above volume was advertised for sale in Cary's catalogue of 1830; it is therefore possible that a copy may yet be preserved. It has been stated that the "authoress was a Miss Julia Beckwith, afterwards Mrs. Hart, of Fredericton, New Brunswick." [*Canadiana*, Vol. II., p. 36.]

9. [1825]. "Wonders of the West, or, A Day at the Falls of Niagara, in 1825;" a poem by a Canadian, 1825. C. Fothergill, Printer, York (Toronto), 46pp., 12mo.

This book is in Mr. Gagnon's possession.

The author was Mr. J. L. Alexander, teacher in the York Grammar School; afterwards incumbent of Saltfleet and Binbrook.

10. [1825]. "Speech in Committee on the bill for conferring civil rights on certain inhabitants of this province." On reverse of the blue paper cover "December 5th, 1825." "The house having resolved itself into a committee upon the bill," etc.

No place or date is given. There is internal evidence that Mr., afterwards Sir John Beverley Robinson, then Attorney General, was the speaker.

This *brochure* of 56 pp., is in the collection of Mr. Gagnon.

11. [1826]. "An abridged view of the Alien Question unmasked." By the Editor of the Canadian *Freeman*. York, U. C., 1826. pp. 16.

The author, Francis Collins, in 1823, was tried for libel on the Attorney-General, afterwards Sir J. B. Robinson. He was sentenced to a fine of £50, imprisonment for one year, and to find security for future good behaviour.

12. [1826]. " The Wandering Rhymer, a fragment with other poetical trifles." York. Printed at the U. C. *Gazette* office, 1826 ; pp. 22, 8vo.

13. [1827]. "The Naturalization Bill, as passed by the House of Assembly and Legislative Council, and reserved for His Majesty's assent. Third Session, ninth Provincial Parliament. Also, the Address of Messrs. Jonas and Charles Jones to the inhabitants of the district of Johnstown and the remarks of ' an Anglo-American Freeholder' thereon." Printed at the *Herald* office, 1827. 13pp.

14. [1827]. "The History of the Destruction of the Colonial Advocate Press by officers of the Provincial Government of Upper Canada, and Law Students of the Attorney & Solicitor-General in open day, and in presence of the Honourable William Allan, a Police Magistrate and collector of the Customs, and Stephen Heward, Esquire, Auditor-General of the colony, by William L. Mackenzie, Editor and proprietor." Part II., York. Printed at the *Colonial Advocate* office, by W. L. Mackenzie, printer to the Honourable the House of Assembly of Upper Canada, 1827. 24pp.

15. [1827]. "A sermon preached at Kingston, Upper Canada, on Sunday, the 25th Day of November, 1827, on occasion of divine service at the opening of St. George's Church, by the Venerable George Okill Stuart, A.M., LL.D., Archdeacon of Kingston, and Missionary of the Society for Propagating the Gospel in Foreign Parts." Published by request. Kingston. Printed by Hugh C. Thompson, 1827. 16pp. 8vo.

In the collection of the late Sheriff Chauveau.

16. [1827]. "A series of reflections on the management of Civic Rule in the town of Kingston, Upper Canada. By an Inhabitant." Kingston. Printed by Hugh C. Thomson, 1827 ; pp., 60., 12mo.

17. [1827]. " Report of the Home District Committee of the Society for Promoting Christian Knowledge. For the year 1827." York, U.C. Printed by R. Stanton ; pp. 10, 8vo.

18. [1827]. "Statement of the affairs of the late Pretended Bank of Upper Canada at Kingston, containing reports of the Commissioners appointed by several Acts of the Provincial Parliament to settle the affairs of the said institution, together with certain other accompanying documents referred to in the report, being Lists of the Stock-Holders, Creditors, Debtors, &c., &c., &c. Reprinted by order of the House of Assembly." York. Printed by William Lyon Mackenzie, at the office of the *Colonial Advocate ;* pp. 48, 8vo.

19. [1828]. "Statement of facts relating to the trespass on the printing press in the possession of Mr. William Lyon M'Kenzie, in June, 1826, addressed to the public generally and particularly to the subscribers and supporters of the *Colonial Advocate,* York." Printed by R. Stanton. 32pp.

The author of this work was Mr. S. P. Jarvis ; it appeared in 1828.

20. [1828.] "The Legislative Black List of Upper Canada, or Official Corruption and Hypocrisy unmasked." York, 1828. 40pp.

Mr. Lindsey, in his " Life of Mackenzie," thus describes this volume: "His 'Legislative Black List,' early commenced and assiduously kept up, contained a short commentary on the divisions that had taken place during the two previous Provincial Parliaments, on prominent and important questions. * * * Compared with electioneering documents of the present day whether in Canada or the States, the 'Black List' was mild and moderate. In publishing Mr. Small's election address, he simply appended to it within brackets 'Printed at the Government Office.'" [I., p. 146.]

21. [1828.] "Letter from the Reverend Egerton Ryerson to the Hon. and Reverend doctor Strachan," published originally in the *Upper Canada Herald*, Kingston, U. C. Printed at the *Herald* Office, 1828. Small 4to. 42pp.

22. [1828.] "Religious Discourses, by the author of Waverley." Kingston, U. C. Printed and published by James Macfarlane, 1828. 16pp., 8vo.

In the collection of the late Sheriff Chauveau.

23. [1828]. "Claims of the Churchmen and Dissenters of Upper Canada brought to the test; in a controversy between several members of the Church of England and a Methodist preacher."

Kingston, U. C. Printed at the *Herald* Office, 1828. 232pp. 8vo.

In the collection of Mr. Gagnon.

24. [1828.] A pamphlet of 11pp. folio, without title, "a letter of Mr. John B. Robinson, Attorney General, to George Hillier, Secretary to the Lieutenant-Governor." York, June 17th, 1828.

Printed at the *Upper Canada Gazette* Office.

The pamphlet is an answer to the statement made in court by Mr. Justice Willis, the first day of term.

This is no place to enter into the now forgotten dispute between Mr. Justice Willis and the Government. At the time, from the excited state of political feeling, the suspension of Mr. Justice Willis by Sir Peregrine Maitland was made a party question, and is so considered to this day.

c

Those who desire a temperate, fair and able narrative of this complicated question, may be referred to Mr. Read's "Lives of the Justices" [pp. 108-117]. What must strike the reader of modern times is the rapidity with which events moved. Mr. Willis presented to the lieutenant-governor, Sir Peregrine Maitland, the royal warrant by which he was appointed judge of the King's Bench, on the 18th of September, 1827. On the 26th of June, 1828, he was removed from his office, the warrant being signed by the lieutenant-governor and the attorney-general. The cause of his removal was his refusal to sit with Mr. Justice Sherwood, without a third judge, on the ground that the court so constituted was illegal. Leave of absence had been granted by the lieutenant-governor to Chief-Justice Campbell, so two judges were only present, when the act set forth that three should hold the court. There had previously been a difference of view, somewhat sharply expressed, between the Justice Willis and the Attorney-General Robinson, as to the manner in which the latter had performed his duty as attorney-general.

The dispute was carried before the privy council. The decision pronounced was, that Mr. Willis had erred in his construction of the statute, and that, notwithstanding the absence of the chief-justice, he should have held the court with Mr. Justice Sherwood. On the other hand, it was held that his dismissal was too summary, and, hence, unwarrantable; that charges should have been formulated against him, so that he might have had the right of reply, and of setting forth the principle on which he had acted.

According to Mr. Read, the antagonism was early created between Mr. Justice Willis and the Attorney-General. The former desired to establish a court of equity, which the

latter constantly opposed.* It is probable that no little of
the friction arose from this circumstance.

25. [1828]. "The formation and constitution of the
York U. C. Bible Society, with the first address of its
members to their Christian friends." York. Printed by
W. L. Mackenzie, at the office of the *Colonial Advocate*,
1828 ; pp. 26, 12mo.

26. [1828]. "Directions to those who raise Tobacco in
this Province." York. Printed by W. L. MacKenzie, at
the office of the *Colonial Advocate*, 1828 ; pp. 16, 12mo.

27. [1828]. "The Charter of the University of King's
College at York, in Upper Canada." Kingston, U.C., 1828.
Reprinted by H. C. Thompson ; pp. 14, 12mo.

28. [1828]. "The Address to Protestant Dissenters,
suited to the present times." Kingston, U.C. Printed
and published (for the author) by H. C. Thompson, and
sold by most Booksellers in the province, 1828; pp. 52, 12mo.

29. [1828]. "Manual of Parliamentary Practice, with
an Appendix containing the Rules of the Legislative Council and House of Assembly of Upper Canada." Compiled,
printed and published by H. C. Thompson, 1828; pp. 92,
8vo.

30. [1829.] "The *Lower Canada Watchman*, Pro
Patria," Kingston, U.C., 1829, 18mo., James Macfarlane,
Printer.

It is formed from the newspaper type of a series of letters
originally published in the Kingston *Chronicle*. It is not
scarce. There is a copy in the excellent library of the well-

* It may be proper to mention, that in less than nine years from
this date the court of chancery was established [4 March, 1837].
the first vice-chancellor being Mr. Jameson. Introducing the
fact, Mr. Read remarks, "The want of a Court of Equity in this
Province had begun to be seriously felt." [p. 193.]

known Abbé Verreault, of Montreal; a copy in the Public Library, Toronto, likewise one in the Parliamentary Library; Mr. Gagnon also has a copy. The type used in the columns of the paper makes up the book. These letters bear the signature T. L. C. W. A second edition contains some supplemental matter. Mr. Bain's copy in the Toronto library has letters 11 and 12, not in the Verreault copy.

The authorship is attributed to Mr. David Chisholme, who arrived in Canada in 1822. Lord Dalhousie was then governor-general, having held the position from the June of the previous year. Chisholme strongly supported the policy of lord Dalhousie, and obtained his confidence. It was the latter who appointed Chisholme clerk of the peace at Three Rivers. Lord Dalhousie remained in Canada until 1828. During the administration of lord Gosford, in November, 1836, Chisholme was dismissed from his office, owing to the hostility felt towards him by the dominant party from his openly expressed opinions. Such as desire to learn the views of the party opposed to the policy of lord Gosford, will find it clearly defined, and with little circumspection of phrase, in the once well-known "Anti-Gallic letters," written in 1835 and 1836 by Adam Thom.

31. [1829.] "Six sermons on the Liturgy of the Church of England." York, U.C., 1829. 16pp.

At this period the writer was the incumbent of Grimsby, the Rev. A. U. Bethune: afterwards bishop of Toronto. [Nov., 1867; Feb., 1879.]

32. [1830.] "A Report of the Case of Sheldon Hawley v. George Hand, Kingston, 1826." A now forgotten law case.

33. [1830.] "Responsible or Parliamentary Government: A political pamphlet." Toronto: 1st ed., 1830; 2nd ed., 1839. 8vo.

The author, Mr. Ogle R. Gowan, an Irishman arrived in Canada in 1829. He was elected to the legislature in 1834, and remained a member of the Parliament of Upper Canada and of the Province of Canada until 1861.

Thus, previous to the work mentioned in "Canadian Archæology" as the first printed book in Upper Canada, those above enumerated preceded it. I repeat the title in this place to make the present list complete.

34. [1832.] "History of the late War between Great Britain and the United States of America, with a retrospective view of the causes from which it originated, collected from the most authentic sources; to which is added an appendix containing public documents, etc., relating to the subject." By David Thompson, late of the Royal Scots, Niagara, U.C. Printed by T. Sewell, Printer, Bookbinder, and Stationer, Market Square, 1832. 300pp. 12mo.

35. [1833.] "The | Constitution | of the | Canadas | adopted by the imperial parliament in the | thirty-first year of the reign of his | Majesty George the III. | and | in the year of our Lord one thousand seven | hundred and ninety-one | Together with the debates thereon | Printed by Joseph Wilson | Hallowell U.C. 1833, pp. 125, 12mo."

Hallowell was the name formerly given to the present town of Picton. According to the account we read in Belden's Historical Atlas, it was the original name west of the bridge. East of the bridge, only, was called Picton, after the distinguished general who fell at Waterloo. Opinion was divided which name should be retained. Finally, it is said against the feeling of the majority, the selection of Picton was made, and the town was so incorporated about 1847. The township of Hallowell was the centre of an United Empire settlement.

36. [1837]. "Observations upon Emigration to Upper

Canada, being the prize essay for which was awarded a gold
medal from the Upper Canada Celtic Society." By Joseph
Neilson. Kingston : Printed at the office of the *Chronicle
and Gazette*, 1837. 74pp., 8vo.

The essay describes the different districts of Upper Canada,
and concludes with a few words of advice to the emigrant.

37. [1840.] "Notes upon Canada and the United States,
from 1832 to 1840, much in a small space, or a great deal in
a little book." By A Traveller. Second Edition. Toronto
(late York), Upper Canada. Printed by Rogers and
Thompson, *Commercial Herald* office, 1840. 184pp. 12mo.

This work is an extraordinary medley of disconnected notes
of matters succeeding each other without any relation.
They bear the mark of being written upon first impression
and without exact inquiry, consequently many are of doubt-
ful accuracy. The book, in its way, is a literary curiosity.
Many facts regarding the province are to be found in this
volume which are not elsewhere preserved. Without
suggesting the least want of good faith or honesty of
purpose on the part of the writer of them, it is difficult to
resist the impression that they must be taken with the
traditional *grano salis*. The author was Mr. Henry Cook
Todd, father of Dr. Alpheus Todd, many years the parliamentary librarian, whose own work I have shortly to record.
He passed through Oxford University, where he acquired
some learning and the taste for collecting books. Possessed
originally of some means, he unfortunately lost much of them
in speculation, and he supplemented the income remaining to
him by aiding in the collection of libraries, and in "coaching"
undergraduates. He came to Canada in 1832 and died in
1862. He was accomplished in many respects, being an
excellent artist. His grandchildren still possess many
of his sketches and pen-and-ink drawings, of great merit.

He was author of the two following works, independently of the one above named :—

(1). "Manual of Orthoepy, on a new plan to render a right pronunciation of words attainable at first sight; with over 2,000 curious notes," 1801. 12mo. London.

(2). "Items (in Life of an Usher) on travel, anecdote, and popular errors," by one in Retirement. 8vo. Quebec. 1855.

38. [1840.] Alpheus Todd, LL.D. "The Practice and Privileges of the Two Houses of Parliament: with an Appendix of Forms." Printed by order of the House of Assembly. 1 vol., 8vo. Toronto, 1840.

Dr. Todd at a later period of his life produced the two important works with which his name is identified, viz. :—

"On Parliamentary Government in England : its origin, development and practical operation." 2 vols., 8vo. London, 1867–9.

2nd Ed., 2 vols., 8vo. London, 1887–9.

"Parliamentary Government in the British Colonies." 1 vol., 8vo. Boston, 1880. 2nd Edition in press.

He has to be specially mentioned as at this date producing a book which has brought honour upon his country. I have, however, appended the two volumes subsequently published, founded upon his first work. Dr. Todd, son of Henry Cook Todd, was born in London, 30th July, 1821, and died in Ottawa, 22nd January, 1884. He was but nineteen years of age when his first book was written, "Practice and Privileges of the Two Houses of Parliament," a remarkable work for so young a man.

The circumstances under which this volume appeared require to be clearly stated It must be distinctly remembered that Dr. Todd was the forerunner in modern times in treating of parliamentary practice. His book was published four years before that of Sir Erskine May. Until this time the standard authority was Hatsell's " Precedents of Proceedings in the House of Commons : with observations." 4 vols. The first edition appeared in 1781, the last in 1818, with some additions by Abbot, Lord Colchester, who had been fifteen years Speaker of the House of Commons. Hatsell himself had been Clerk of the House, from which office he retired in 1797. He died in 1820.

Dr. Todd's second, and indeed his chief book, has obtained for him a European reputation. It has been translated into German and Italian, and is held in the highest esteem in the mother country, which Todd doubtless considered as the greatest honour he could obtain. His third book, on " Parliamentary Government in the Colonies," has gained equally favourable consideration both at home and in the Dominion. It is the text-book of the Toronto University.

Those imperial writers, constantly ready to recognize the most ephemeral productions of the United States, as of astounding merit, and who pass by with cold mention, more often in silence, any effort of the provincial intellect, will do well to remember that the first authoritative book on parliamentary law was produced in Canada in 1840, four years before any modern English writer had approached the subject. There are, fortunately, writers in the London press of a different stamp, who kindly and generously recognize what they conceive to be merit, whatever the latitude and longitude at which it is displayed. Unfortunately, such as these are not frequently met. Those not in the category would do well to read the records of the American revolution of a century back. The real grievance was not the Stamp Act, and all the misrepresentation which has been written about the tyranny of the home government. It was the misapprehension and the failure to do justice to the colonial intellect which estranged men like Jefferson, Samuel Adams, and Madison, who learned from personal sentiment to entertain an unextinguishable hatred to England. What was the experience in the two cases I am considering? Sir Erskine May received many honours, and deservedly so, dying as Lord Farnborough in 1886. Dr. Todd remained unnoticed for years by the London journalist and the home government. The consideration which he received late in life, the degree of LL.D., *honoris causa*, was conferred by Queen's University. Owing to the intervention of Lord Lorne, himself a man of letters, always foremost in the recognition of merit, and who has left behind him in Canada the record of his constant sympathy with art and literature in connection with his high statesmanlike abilities, Dr. Todd received the imperial distinction of a C.M.G. It is, moreover, well known that in the Dominion, his honest expression of opinion regarding the Letellier question in the province of Quebec, an opinion which remains unimpeachable, led to an expression of petulant bad feeling on the part of men in power in Canada, which one day will be more fully related. It was the reward he received from the Canadian Government.

Some reprints of known works were early published, viz.:—

1. [1823]. " The True-Born Englishman ; a Political Satyr " [*sic*]. By Daniel DeFoe. Reprinted from the old edition, 1823 ; pp. 32, 12mo.

2. [1823]. " The Canadian's Right, the same as the Englishman's.—A Dialogue between a Barrister-at-Law and a Juryman, setting forth the Antiquity, excellent design, use, office and just privileges of Juries, By the Law of England. First written by Sir John Hawles, Knight, Solicitor-General to William III." York, U.C. Now republished by Charles Fothergill, Esq., 1823 ; pp. 52, 12mo.

3. [1831.] "The Life and Actions of Alexander the Great," by the Rev. J. Williams, Vicar of Lampeter. First Canada edition, Niagara, 1831. 200pp. in 8vo.

4. [1831.] "The Life of Mahomed, Founder of the Religion of Islam and of the Empire of the Saracens," by the Rev. Geo. Bush. First Canada edition, Niagara, 1831. 112pp. in 8vo.

5. [1831.] Chapman's reprint of Murray's Family Library. "The Life of Lord Nelson," by Robert Southey, Esq., LL.D., Poet Laureate, etc., etc. First Canada edition, Niagara, 1831. 140pp. in 8vo.

6. [1832.] "The Life of Lord Byron," by John Galt, Esq., Niagara : Henry Chapman, publisher. Samuel Heron, printer, 1831. 200pp. in 8vo.

I append a list of the several works published outside of the territory of Canada, from the period succeeding the close of the American war of 1783 and the establishment of Upper Canada, to the date of the union of the provinces, 11th February, 1841. The names of only those writers are given, who considered the economic condition, the politics, the history of the province, and of those who, in the narrative of their travels, have furnished information concerning the period which they represent. The names not included are writers of sermons, religious and controversial books ; the narratives of personal adventure, unless of historic interest ; works of fiction, poems, laudatory biography, papers on abstract science not directly related to Canada, the arraignment of slavery, and such works as may be classed under the title of general literature.

I likewise leave unnoticed the pamphlets which have

appeared from time to time upon Canadian affairs. From about 1835 to the return home of Lord Durham in 1838, even to a later date, they are very numerous, and may be said to form in themselves a minor source of information apart from the works which I have named. It is not impossible that at some future period a catalogue of them may be attempted.

Many of the volumes catalogued have long been forgotten, or, if at all read, it is owing to the record of some minor local fact of little general value. I consider, however, that this list will not be disdained by the historical student. I cannot hope that it will be found to be perfect. A great many names, however, are presented according to date, and it will be a comparatively easy matter in the future to supplement the list, as better information will admit. The calendar is submitted with this explanation. Generally speaking, I have appended some explanatory remarks concerning the volumes to which I could obtain access, and I trust they will not be held to be entirely valueless. Where I fail to do so, it has been from my inability to discover the books unnoticed.

Jean-François, Marquis de Chastellux. "Voyages dans L'Amérique Septentrionale, dans les années, 1780, 1781, et 1782." Paris, Prault, 1788. 2 vols. 8vo.

In English: "Travels in North America in the years 1780, 1781 and 1782, by the Marquis de Chastellux, one of the forty members of the French Academy, and Major-General in the French Army, serving under the Count of Rochambeau. Translated from the French by an English gentleman who resided in America at that period. With notes by the translator." London, 1777.

I mention this work, being one of the earliest of this date. It has, however, no bearing upon Canada. It is the diary of two journeys;

one, from Newport to Philadelphia, to Saratoga and to Portsmouth in New Hampshire; the second in Virginia. It contains information relative to the war of independence and some of the principal actors in it.

George Cartwright. "A Journal of Transactions and Events during a residence of nearly sixteen years on the coast of Labrador. Containing many interesting particulars both of the country and its inhabitants not hitherto known. Illustrated with proper charts." Newark, 1792. 3 vols. 4to.

Captain Cartwright, in a short biography of his life, tells us that he served in India, and was aide-de-camp to the celebrated Marquis of Granby. Afterwards, he obtained a company in the 37th regiment, was present at Minorca, and suffered from the ague; and, finally, retired on half-pay in 1770. On 17th May, 1770, he sailed for Newfoundland to obtain possession of the vessel in which the enterprise of trading in Labrador was to be carried out.

There is a great deal of information in these three volumes, but it has to be sought for; the narrative is often tedious, and dwells upon much which has little interest.

Thomas Anbury. "Travels through the interior parts of America during the course of the last War. In a series of Letters, by an Officer to his friends." London, 1789; 2nd edition, 1791. 2 vols., 8vo.

Translated by P. L. Lebas, Paris, 1790, afterwards by M. Noel of the College of Louis-le-Grand. Paris, 1793.

This work is generally described under the name of Anbury. Although the name does not appear on the title page, it is given as Anbury in the dedication to Lord Harrington. There are several pages of subscribers. The author was an ensign of the 24th, and he collected in these two volumes the letters written by him during his stay in America. He landed in Quebec in October, 1776, and being a keen observer of what he saw, gives us a pleasantly written narrative of the opinions he formed of Canada at that time. The following year he took part in Burgoyne's unfortunate expedition, and after the surrender at Saratoga, was sent to Cambridge, not far from Boston. He was afterwards removed to Winchester, in

Virginia. In 1781 he obtained his liberty and reached New York. His letters, while giving a narrative of his own experience, record the impressions he formed of the country during the three years he passed there.

P. Campbell. "Travels in the interior inhabited parts of North America in the years 1791 and 1792." In which is given an account of the manners and customs of the Indians, and the present war between them and the Federal States, the mode of life and system of farming among the new settlers of both Canadas, New York, New England, New Brunswick and Nova Scotia, interspersed with anecdotes of people, observations on the soil, natural productions and political situation of these countries. Illustrated with copper plates." Edinburgh, 1793.

A curious narrative of the travels of a Highlander through some of the lately settled districts of Canada. The book can still be read with interest, owing to the relation of much not to be found elsewhere. At Burlington he passed three weeks with Brandt. A great-grand-daughter of Mr. Campbell is still living at Fort Erie.

Thomas Cooper. "Some information respecting America, collected by Thomas Cooper, late of Manchester." London, 1794. 8vo.

In French. "Renseignements sur l'Amerique Anglaise; traduit de l'Anglais." Paris, 1795. 8vo.

This book has relation only to the United States. There is an appendix of some value bearing upon the migration of summer and winter birds of passage.

Charles Grant, Vicomte de Vaux. "Adressé à toutes les puissances de l'Europe sur l'état présent et futur de la noblesse, et du clergé Français. Particulièrement au Gouvernement Britannique, sur les moyens d'assurer à ces deux corps l'existence la plus convenable aux circonstances, moyennant un plan d'établissements dans le Canada, les plus avantangenx possibles, soit au Commerce Britannique, soit aux Loyalistes." Londres, 1794. pp. 109.

This work was an appeal made in England to aid the French *noblesse* and ecclesiastics, driven from France at the period of the revolution. One proposal being to establish them in Canada, four commissioners, French ecclesiastics, were sent to Quebec, in 1792, to make an examination as to the character and condition of the province. Their report, written in Quebec in the month of October, is here given. It contains much information, particularly as to the early settlements on Lake Ontario, and gives some detail, even, with regard to the Bay of Chaleurs.

Several emigrants of French royalist families arrived in Canada in 1798, under M. de Puisaye. The subject is narrated at some length by Dr. Brymner, in his Report Canadian Archives of 1888 [p. XXVI., ap. 85] to which the reader is referred.

"A letter descriptive of the different settlements in the Province of Upper Canada." London, 1795.

This volume of 27 pages give the fullest picture we possess of the condition of the Province in 1794. It is written in the form of a letter from New York, but having been published in London, it may be assumed that this method was followed as a matter of convenience, and it is not impossible that it had an official origin. It commences by stating that vessels sailed from Oswego to Niagara, Kingston and other ports on Lake Ontario, but that generally settlers followed the south shore to Niagara in the same open boats in which they had arrived, plainly having in view such as had ascended the Saint Lawrence. Settlement is described as extending to lake Saint Francis; vessels, however, seldom went below Kingston. Even at that date the quarries in the neighbourhood were held of value. The most flourishing settlements were to be found round the bay of Quinté. The soil was so easily worked, that without any other cultivation but that of the iron-toothed harrow, it produced from one to three crops of from 20 to 30 bushels of wheat to the acre. The whole bay at this date had "the appearance of a beautiful old settled country." Lake Ontario was then plentifully supplied with fish at all seasons of the year. In the winter, quantities of white fish were caught by seines from two to six lbs. in weight. Sturgeon, bass and other species were in great plenty. Salmon was taken in all the creeks running into the lake. The land around Newark (Niagara) was inhabited for fifty miles. The writer claims to have been acquainted with Mr., afterwards Sir David Smith, the surveyor general, and to have had access to his notes. Queenston, seven miles above Niagara, was the spot where vessels were unloaded and "took in furs collected from three to one thousand five hundred miles back." The upper landing-place was at Chippewa Creek ; the portage was an increasing source of wealth to the farmers for many miles around. The cost of transport was one shilling and eightpence N.Y. currency per cwt. From Chippewa the merchandise was carried by *bateaux* on lake Erie to Detroit and Michillimackinac.

Hamilton had just been located "a small town" at the head of lake Ontario, a central place between Newark and York, "called by the natives Toronto," to Detroit. A road of twenty miles is "cut out" to the Grand river, which it crosses about fifty miles above the entrance into lake Erie, and continues to the river La Tranche, now called the Thames. Settlements were being made between Hamilton and Niagara, and partial ones along the river Thames to the extent of eighty or ninety miles. The town of York (Toronto) was in great forwardness, and a road cut to lake Simcoe. Settlement was commencing on this line of road, and on the east side one hundred German families had established themselves in rear of these lots. They had arrived in the summer of 1794, "furnished with everything necessary to make their situation comfortable. They are sustained by a company who supply them with teams, utensils and provisions."

The settlement was begun by a few disbanded troops after the peace of 1783. As in the United States the opinion prevailed that the country was entirely under military control, but few emigrants arrived. When it, however, became known that a civil government was established under a happily-formed constitution, numbers left the United States to live under the British flag. They were among the most respectable of the inhabitants. Some arrived in waggons even from North Carolina to the mouth of the Genesee river. As the open road did not extend beyond this spot, they were trans-ported in boats to the mouth of the Niagara river, and thence by boat to York. Large grants of land were also being made to the Royalists.

The writer highly commends the wisdom of dividing Canada into the then two provinces. I do not wish here to enter into that question, for I have to do so in another place. One fact is very evident in the then condition of the country with its imperfect roads, it would have been simply impossible for members representing the early settlements of Upper Canada to have found their way to a legislative assembly holding its meetings in Quebec. A great deal has been written on this point without reflection; the same may be said with regard to the abandonment of the territory south and west of lake Erie, now the states of Ohio, Michigan and Illinois. To me it appears it would have been impossible to have retained the territory without very strong military posts; and they could only have been maintained at a great cost of men and money, the possession of which ultimately would have been the cause of another war from the aggressive spirit of the border population of the United States. Modern writers set out of view that for some years after the peace of Versailles, war with the United States from the failure on the part of that government to observe the treaties with regard to Canada and British interests, was for a long time a matter of no slight probability, and that it was greatly owing to the honest wisdom of Washington, and those who sustained him, that hostilities were avoided.

We learn that the land rights of Indians were extinguished by fair and just purchase, as the population of the country required additional territory. It is one of the most honourable facts of Canadian history, that this policy has never been departed from, and that it prevails to this day. The writer of the book describes the political institutions of the country, and much of its interior economy. We learn from him that *bateaux* of 25 barrels bulk, with four men, reached Kingston from Montreal in six to eight days, and returned in three days, with furs, potash and other produce. He is one of the few who do not rise to enthusiasm about the Falls of Niagara, although by no means a matter-of-fact personage. He informs us that a quantity of British goods found their way to the Mississippi; and he speaks of Sir Alexander Mackenzie's expedition to the Pacific Ocean as worthy of comment. This unpretentious volume is one of the most useful which we possess of this class.

De La Rochefoucault-Liancour. "Voyage dans les Etats-

Unis de l'Amérique en 1795 et 1797. Enrichi de plusieurs cartes." Paris, 1798. 8 vols. in 8vo.

"Travels through the United States of North America, the country of the Iroquois and Upper Canada in the years 1795, 1796, and 1797, with an authentic account of Lower Canada. Translated from the French [with Maps]." London, 1800. Second edition. 4 vols., 4to.

The duc de Rochefoucault was born in 1747, and died in 1829. His work represents the condition of the agriculture, manufactures and commerce of the period. He likewise gives his impressions of the national life and domestic habits of the people. De Rochefoucault remained nearly three years in the United States.

He crossed the Niagara river on the 20th of June, 1795, two miles below fort Erie. He was received by the captain of a frigate in command of the lakes, on the part of Governor Simcoe, with due ceremony. Fort Erie had a small garrison of the 5th regiment. There were some troops at fort Chippewa; the head-quarters of the regiment was at Niagara. Detroit and the western forts were held by the 25th; these frontier forts not having been given over to the United States. He found specie, hard money, very scarce, business being carried on by paper notes, some of which were as low as two pence. De Rochefoucault was one of the first to give an elaborate description of the Falls. At Niagara he met Governor Simcoe, who shewed him lord Dorchester's order, not to allow any foreigner to enter Lower Canada, and Simcoe was obliged to apply to lord Dorchester at Kingston for a passport for him to do so. The duke thus remained some time with Simcoe, in the hope of obtaining this permission. He gives us the most favourable impression of the governor and his wife, a woman of sense and capacity, who acted as her husband's private secretary, and aided in the preparation of maps. He describes with ability the institutions and condition of Upper Canada; he has, however, some extraordinary views concerning the Indians. He relates that 50,000 were prepared, in case of war, to take the British side, all of whom had taken an oath not to leave a scalp on any "American" they fell in with.

M. de Rochefoucault was not permitted to enter Lower Canada.

D

It was not, however, a matter of whim that enforced the prohibition; the relations between the United States and Great Britain were then very delicate, and events were assuming an ominous outlook. The refusal to allow de Rochefoucault to visit Lower Canada by the Saint Lawrence was on the theory that he was acting in the interest of the United States, for if war broke out, Canada would have been the battle-field. Great Britain was dissatisfied with the non-fulfilment of Articles IV. and VI. of the Treaty of Versailles, in 1783, which provided for the restitution of all estates, rights and properties belonging to British subjects. Article V. provided that Congress should recommend the States to carry out these conditions. At a subsequent date, Jefferson characteristically declared that all the United States had agreed to was, to recommend to the states that the conditions should be observed, but with no expectation that the recommendation would be carried out. On all sides every difficulty was thrown in the way of fulfilling these obligations. Great Britain therefore declared that these articles not being observed, its government could not be held to the fulfilment of the obligation to surrender the frontier forts. It was, indeed, not until 1796 that the transfer was made.

The answer arrived on the 22nd of July, prohibiting a visit to Lower Canada. We can understand that these memoirs do not contain a flattering portrait of lord Dorchester. The remarks bearing upon Canada are worthy of attention and contain much information. Not being allowed to descend the Saint Lawrence, the duke proceeded to Oswego, and from that spot continued his travels in the United States.

J. C. Ogden. "A tour through Upper and Lower Canada. By a citizen of the United States. Containing a view of the present state of religion, learning, commerce, agriculture, colonization, customs, and manners among the English, French, and Indian Settlements." Lichfield, 1797. 12mo.

2nd Edition. Wilmington, 1800, by John. C. Ogden, of the Episcopal Church.

The author, son-in-law of General David Wooster, resided in New Haven, 1771–85. Subsequently, he was the incumbent of the episcopal church at Portsmouth, N.H. The description of Upper Canada, forming a separate letter of 26 pages, is full of interest, shewing the author's strong sympathies with the royalists.

Isaac Weld. "Travels through the States of North America and the Provinces of Upper and Lower Canada during the years 1795, 1796 and 1797." London. 2nd Edition, 1799. 2 vols., 8vo.

Translated, Paris, 1799. 3 vols., 8vo.

Mr. Weld entered Canada by lake Champlain and made his way to Montreal and to Quebec. The navigation of the lake was not then a pleasant matter, being made in ten-ton boats, which in bad weather sought shelter. Weld gives a picturesque account of the country wherever he travels, and is a shrewd observer of manners and social habits. As we read the picture of those days we see how much, in some respects, remains unchanged. Our present mode of travel, however, is, in fact as in date, a century in advance ; the navigation of the Saint Lawrence is not now undertaken in a *bateau* as in the time of Weld. The notes of his journey to Quebec record the time it then occupied. He left Montreal on the 1st day of August, at eleven, and at five arrived at Sorel. The next morning he proceeded on his journey and reached Batiscan, where he slept. The third night he passed at Saint Augustin. On the fourth morning he arrived at Quebec. The usual time, remarks Weld, does not exceed two days, when the wind is fair and tide favourable. Weld ascended the Saint Lawrence, stopping at Kingston, the Niagara Falls and Newark [Niagara]. There was then mention of moving the seat of government elsewhere, and of cutting a canal round the portage : the forerunner of the scheme of the Welland Canal. Weld was at Niagara in September, 1796, after the posts had been ceded to the United States : Oswegatchie [Ogdensburg], Oswego, Niagara, Detroit and Michillimackinac. He went as far as Malden, on the Detroit River, where he took leave of Canada.

Sir Alexander Mackenzie. "Voyages from Montreal on the River St. Lawrence, through the continent of North America, to the Frozen and Pacific Oceans, in the years 1789 and 1793 ; with a preliminary account of the rise, progress,

and present state of the Fur Trade of that country."
Illustrated with Maps. London, 1801. 1 vol. 8vo.
Philadelphia, 1802. 1 vol. 8vo.

Sir Alexander Mackenzie was the first white man to reach the
Arctic Ocean, by the river which bears his name, and the first who
crossed the Rocky Mountains and reached the Pacific. There are
few more valuable contributions to the history of travel, and his
narrative is still read and held in the highest estimation.

"Sketch of His Majesty's province of Upper Canada,"
by D'Arcy Boulton, Barrister-at-Law. London, 1805. 4to.

This quarto volume is dedicated to the King [George III.]. It
is the recommendation of Upper Canada as a field of emigration to
the British settler. The opening sentence is typical of the tone of
the book. "An honest man, with industry, may live there in
greater ease and with less labour than in any part of the continent
with which I am acquainted." The volume is valuable for the
information it gives of the period. It describes the districts and
character of the settlements, and the local detail it furnishes will
be invaluable to the county historian. The appendix contains an
account of the several townships, alphabetically arranged.

George Heriot. "Travels through the Canadas, containing a description of the picturesque scenery on some of the
Rivers and Lakes; with an account of the productions,
commerce, and inhabitants of those Provinces: to which is
subjoined a comparative view of the manners and customs
of several of the Indian Nations of North and South
America. Illustrated with a map and numerous engravings,
from drawings made at the several places by the author."
London, 1807. 4to.

On the appearance of this work, exception was taken to the somewhat minute geographical description of the second part. It is
this feature of the narrative which to-day gives any value to the
work with the local antiquary. Mr. Heriot was deputy postmaster-
general of British North America.

Hugh Gray. "Letters from Canada, written during a residence there in the years 1806, 1807, and 1808, shewing the present state of Canada, its productions, trade, commercial, and political relations. Illustrative of the laws and manners of the people and the peculiarities of the country and climate. Exhibiting also the commercial importance of Nova Scotia, New Brunswick, and Cape Breton ; and their increasing ability, in conjunction with Canada, to furnish the necessary supplies of Lumber and provisions to our West India Islands." London, 1809. 8vo. 2nd Edition, 1814.

This volume is evidently the result of much study and reflection. While it considers the resources and capabilities of the province, it relates sufficient of its history to admit of political speculation. Mr. Gray looked upon the division of Canada into two provinces as having been unwise, and recommended their re-union as a matter easy of accomplishment.

Alexander Henry. "Travels and Adventures in Canada and in the Indian Territories, between the years 1760 and 1776." New York, 1809. 8vo.

It is to Henry's narrative that we are indebted to a knowledge of the seizure of the fort at Michillimackinac in 1763 by the Indians. Independently of the account of this event, and the interest connected with Henry's personal career, the work is valuable as a picture of the times and the description of the customs and manners of both the Indian and the Indian traders.

John Mills Jackson. "A View of the political Situation of the province of Upper Canada, in North America ; in which her physical capacity is stated ; the means of diminishing her burden, increasing her value, and securing her connection to Great Britain, are fully considered." London, 1809. 8vo.

Mr. Jackson inherited a tract of land in the province of Quebec, and visited Lower Canada to investigate his title. He proceeded to Upper Canada, and was so much pleased with what he saw, that he determined to purchase property and settle there. Subsequently, considering "neither his person nor property secure," he relinquished the project. With this feeling he published the volume. He complains of the mode in which, in the days of Governor Simcoe and Mr. Russell, grants of land had been obtained, and of the exorbitant fees exacted. Indeed, he calls in question the whole system of land grants ; he arraigns the courts of law ; he defends Mr. Justice Thorpe, and pronounces Governor Gore's conduct to him to be unjust ; he speaks of the "ruinous expenditure and mismanagement of the public money ;" he appeals on these matters to the Imperial Parliament. The appendix contains several documents not without importance.

John Lambert. "Travels through Canada and the United States of North America, in the years 1806, 1807 and 1808. To which are added, biographical notices and anecdotes of some of the leading characters in the United States :" with a map and numerous engravings. London, 1st Edition, 2 vols., 1810 ; 2nd Ed., 2 vols., 1813 ; 3rd Ed., 2 vols., corrected and improved, 1816.

The first volume is devoted to Canada, the second to the United States. Lambert landed at Quebec in October, 1806. He furnishes a picture of the place of that date, and describes the social manners, dress and political events which were happening, with more than the usual care bestowed by the passing traveller. Much of his historical narrative, however, is not in accordance with fact, having been disproved by authentic documents. From Quebec he visited Three Rivers and Montreal, and ascending Lake Champlain entered the United States. Lambert remained at Quebec from November, 1806, to August, 1807. He came back to Canada in 1808, in order to obtain a passage home. We learn from this work that at this date, both at Quebec and Montreal, the theatre had been established and performances periodically given. His account does not suggest that the acting was of a high order.

M. Smith. "A Geographical View of the Province of Upper Canada, and promiscuous remarks upon the Government ; in 2 parts, with an appendix : containing a complete description of Niagara Falls, and remarks relative to the situation of the Inhabitants respecting the War." Philadelphia, 1813. pp. 118. 12mo.

This book reached a 5th Edition. The title of the 4th and 5th editions was changed to :—

"A Geographical View of the British possessions in North America, comprehending Nova Scotia, New Brunswick, New Britain, Lower and Upper Canada, with all the country to the Frozen Sea, on the North and Pacific Ocean on the West ; with an appendix containing a concise history of the war in Canada to the date of this volume." By M. Smith, author of the "View of Upper Canada." Baltimore, 1814. 6th Edition, Lexington, 1816.

New Britain was the name given to that part of Labrador situate between the 59th and 65th degrees of latitude.

The book is of value from giving a description of the social and political conditions of Upper Canada in the years of war from 1812 to 1814, from the standing-point of a United States citizen.

Mr. M. Smith tells us in his preface that in 1812 he had obtained permission of lieut.-governor Gore to publish the volume, when war was declared by the United States government. Being a citizen of the republic and not being willing to take the oath of allegiance, he obtained passports for his own country. His MSS. having been taken from him before he left Canada, he was forced to supply their place from his rough notes.

One is somewhat puzzled to explain the publication of the volume under such conditions at this date, unless on the theory that the publishers considered it advisable to furnish information concerning the country to the north so soon to be a prey to the conqueror !

Sir David William Smyth, Bart. " A Short Topographical description of His Majesty's Province of Upper Canada, in North America. To which is added a Provincial Gazetteer." London, 1799. pp. 166. 8vo. 2nd Edition, Do. 1813. pp. 123. 8vo.

The following remarks are appended : " The accompanying Notes and Gazetteer were drawn up by David William Symth, the very able Surveyor-General of the province of Upper Canada, at the desire of Major-General Simcoe, on the plan of those of the late Captain Hutchins for the River Ohio and the countries adjacent."

The copy in the Parliamentary Library is the second edition, "revised and corrected by Francis Gore, Esq., Lieut.-Governor." London, 1813.

The work is valuable from the statistical information it furnishes.

Hon. Jonathan Sewell, LL.D. "A Plan for the Federal Union of the British Provinces in North America." London, 1814.

"On the Advantages of Opening the River St. Lawrence to the Commerce of the World." Do. 1814.

Mr. Sewell was afterwards Chief Justice of Lower Canada.

David Anderson. "Canada : or a view of the importance of the British-American Colonies, shewing their Extensive and Improveable Resources, and pointing out the great and unprecedented advantages which have been allowed to the Americans over our own colonists ; together with the great sacrifices which have been made by our late commercial regulations of the commerce and the carrying trade of Great Britain to the United States," &c., &c. London, 1814. 8vo.

The declared object of this work was to shew the importance of the Canadas, with a view to adequate measures being taken for their defence ; and in condemnation of the policy by which the interests of British ship owners and North American colonists had been sacrificed to the United States. The writer had passed several years in British North America. The work is written in the interest of the carrying trade, and is confined to the investigation of the subjects which the inquiry suggests.

J. Melish. "Military documents concerning the Operations of the British Army under General Wolfe in 1759–60, and concerning the War of 1812." Philadelphia, 1814. 8vo.

"Travels in the United States of America in the years 1806 and 1807, and 1809, 1810 and 1811, including an account of passages between America and Britain, and Travels through various parts of Great Britain, Ireland and Upper Canada." Illustrated by eight maps. 2 vols. Philadelphia, 1812, 1818. London, 1818. Dublin, 1818. German edition, Weimar, 1819. 8vo.

This work is mentioned owing to its having been included in the catalogue of works bearing upon Canada. The author, who had served an apprenticeship in Glasgow, in 1806 resolved to commence business on his own account, and in this year sailed to the United States. We learn (p. 497) that he never crossed the Niagara river from Lewiston to Queenston, "the wind was blowing so strong." He, however, gave five pages of the information with regard to Canada which he could gather from books. The volume, in view of Canada, is without the least importance. The text suggests that the writer's sympathy with the United States was of no limited character.

John Eardley-Wilmot, F.R.S. "Historical View of the Commission for Inquiring into the losses, services and claims of the American Loyalists, at the close of the War between Great Britain and her Colonies in 1783 ; with an account of the compensation granted to them by Parliament in 1785 and 1788." London, 1815. 8vo.

This work is important for reference in questions affecting the treatment of the American loyalists. It must always be referred to with great interest by the descendants of the U. E. loyalist families who first came to Canada. It enters into the histories of Articles IV., V., VI., of the Treaty of Versailles, by which the rights of the royalists were protected. The author contends that the "utmost possible pains were taken to procure more substantial Terms for the Loyalists" . . . "further, that the Treaty was on the point of breaking off on this account alone."

Joseph Bouchette, Lieut.-Colonel.  (1.) "A Topographical description of the Province of Lower Canada, with remarks upon Upper Canada, and on the relative connection of both provinces with the United States of America." London, 1815. R. 8vo. Plates 17. Also in French.

(2.) "The British Dominions in North America, or a topographical and statistical description of the Provinces of Lower and Upper Canada, New Brunswick, Nova Scotia, the islands of Newfoundland, Prince Edward and Cape Breton, including considerations on land granting and emigration, and a Topographical Dictionary of Lower Canada ; to which are annexed statistical tables and tables of distances." Published with the author's maps of Lower Canada, in consequence of a vote of the Provincial Legislature. Embellished with vignettes, views, landscapes, plans of towns, harbours, &c.; containing also a copious appendix. London, 1831.  3 vols. 4to.

Colonel Bouchette was at this period surveyor-general of Lower Canada, and, accordingly, he had access to maps, documents and official reports, which to a great extent assured the accuracy of his work. His volumes, consequently at the time, were of the greatest value, and long remained the text book of the province. They contain a representative view of the Dominion at that date. They are often referred to, and are to be found in every library. Colonel Bouchette's careful and conscientious work remains an admirable example to all who desire to write upon the subject in modern times.

Joseph Sansom.  "Sketches of Lower Canada, historical and descriptive ; with the Author's Recollections of the soil and aspect, the morals, habits and religious institutions of that isolated country; during a Tour to Quebec, in the month of July, 1817." New York, 1817.  12mo.

This volume, dedicated to DeWitt Clinton, is a short record of the travels of an United States citizen.  It is the tourist's ordinary narrative, of no interest at present. He tells, however, that at that date salmon were plentiful in the Jacques Cartier River.

John Lewis Thomson. "Historical Sketches of the late War between the United States and Great Britain, blended with anecdotes illustrative of the Individual Bravery of the American Sailors, Soldiers and Citizens ; embellished with Portraits of the most distinguished Naval and Military Officers : and accompanied by Views of Several Sieges and Engagements." Philadelphia. 12mo. 1st Edition, 1816. 5th Edition, 1818.

This work is the history of the war of 1812, by a United States citizen. Its title suggests its character.

Lieut. Edward Chappell. "Narrative of a voyage to Hudson's Bay in His Majesty's Ship 'Rosamund'; containing some account of the North Eastern coast of America, and of the Tribes inhabiting that remote region." London, 1817. 8vo.

"Voyage to Newfoundland and the Southern Coast of Labrador, of which countries no account has been published since the reign of Queen Elizabeth." London, 1818. 8vo.

The former is a narrative of a voyage to York factory. Containing much information, the book is useful for general reference ; it specially relates the voyage to Hudson's Bay of La Perouse in 1782 with a line of battle ship and two frigates. With this force he expected to capture the company's ships in their annual voyage with their rich cargo of furs and oil. Both of these vessels eluded his attack and escaped. La Perouse, angered at his want of success, burned York factory. Lieut. Chappel proceeded some distance up Hayes' River. He was the first, I believe, who gave a map of the route by the Nelson River to Lake Winnipeg, made from the explorations of Mr. William Hillier, a master in the royal navy.

Francis Hall, Lieut. 14th Light Dragoons. "Travels in Canada and the United States in 1816 and 1817." London, 1818. 8vo.

Mr. Hall arrived in winter, and in the following July proceeded to Kamouraska, crossed to Malbaie and returned to Quebec. The narrative is not very lively, but we read names we meet at this day. He returned to Montreal and reached Kingston, where he crossed to Sackett's Harbour and pursued his travels in the United States.

John Palmer. "Journal of Travels in the United States of North America and Lower Canada, performed in the year 1817; containing particulars relating to the prices of land and provisions, remarks on the country and people, interesting anecdotes, and an account of the commerce, trade and present state of Washington, New York, Philadelphia, Boston, Baltimore, Albany, Cincinnati, Pittsburgh, Lexington, Quebec, Montreal, &c. To which are added a description of Ohio, Indiana, Illinois and Missouri, and a variety of other useful information, &c." [With a map.] London, 1818. 8vo.

About thirty pages only of this volume are devoted to Canada. Palmer was present at a buffalo baiting. There were seven bull dogs brought against the male and female buffalo. The dogs were easily beaten off by the male. Both the poor brutes bore the signs of many such encounters. He also describes a *charivari* which took place after a M. Ballet, an elderly member of the House of Assembly, had married his maid. The unfortunate husband endeavoured to resist, but, finally, had to pay the tax for the poor, which his riotous visitors exacted.

Thomas, Earl of Selkirk. (1.) "Sketch of the British Fur Trade in North America, with observations relative to the North-West Company of Montreal." London, 1816. pp. 130. 8vo. New York, 1818. In French, Montreal, 1819.

(2.) "A letter to the Earl of Liverpool from the Earl of Selkirk, accompanied by a Correspondence with the Colonial Department (in the years 1817, 1818, 1819), on the subject of the Red River Settlement in North America." London, 1819. pp. 224. 8vo. Printed for private distribution only.

The Earl of Selkirk will always be remembered in Canadian history as the founder of the Red River Settlement in 1817. His career in the North-West is an important chapter of history, marked by difficulty and bloodshed, concerning which much has been published. The several memoirs on the subject, printed by Selkirk at the time, were for private circulation only. It was not until the union of the Hudson's Bay and the North-West Companies, in 1821, that peace was assured, and the settlement was continued under certain limitations.

H. B. Frearon. "Sketches in America." 1818. 8vo.

This work has reference only to the United States. The author arrived in New York 5th August, 1817, and left for England May 10th, 1818, having made the tour of the Eastern and Western States.

John Douglas. "Medical Topography of Upper Canada." London, 1819.

The author served as assistant surgeon in the 8th regiment until 1816. I have not seen this work.

Gilbert, J. Hunt. "The late War between the United States and Great Britain, from June, 1812, to February, 1815, written in the ancient historical style." 3rd Edition. New York, 1819.

The narrative is carried on in chapter and verse in the phraseology of the Bible.

There is another rare work of this character in the Parliamentary Library at Ottawa :—

"The History of the American Revolution in Scripture style, to which is added the Declaration of Independence, the Constitution of the United States of America, and the interesting farewell address of General Washington." Frederick County, Md. Printed and published by Matthew Bartgis at Pleasant Dale Paper Mill, 1823.

This book has been attributed to Mr. R. Snowdens.

Charles Frederick Grece. "Facts and Observations

respecting Canada and the United States of America, affording a comparative view of the inducements to Emigration presented to those countries. To which is added an appendix of Practical Instructions to Emigrant Settlers in the British Colonies." London, 1819. pp. xv. and 172. 8vo.

The design of this book was to give a view of the agricultural condition of the province, the cost of clearing land, and to set forth the circumstances under which an emigrant should endeavour to establish himself. Many details and much general information are given. This book is a representation of Canada of half a century back, considered from the author's point of view.

E. Mackenzie. "An Historical, Topographical and Descriptive View of the United States of America and of Upper and Lower Canada; with an Appendix, containing a brief and comprehensive sketch of the present state of Mexico and South America; and also of the Native Tribes of the New World." 2nd Edition. Newcastle-upon-Tyne, 1819. 8vo. With maps and engravings.

The allusion to Canada is very brief ; the work appears to have been compiled from the statements of previous writers rather than from personal observation.

Benjamin Silliman. "Remarks made on a Short Tour between Hartford and Quebec, in the autumn of 1819." New Haven, 1820. 12mo.

Mr. Silliman entered Canada by Lake Champlain, and visited Montreal and Quebec. It is the record of a journey made by a man of education. It is pleasantly written and attracted attention at the time, but to-day it is without interest.

Gabriel Franchère. "Relation d'un Voyage à la côté du Nord-Ouest de l'Amérique Septentrionale dans les années 1810, 11, 12, 13 et 14." Montréal, 1820. 8vo.

From the place of publication the volume may at first be considered as belonging to Quebec bibliography. The narrative has, however, no relation to that province. Franchère was one of several Canadians who entered into the service of the Pacific Fur Company, the principal personage of which was Mr. John Jacob Astor. They proceeded to Fort Astoria on the Pacific. The Company eventually sold their property to the North-West Company of Canada. Franchère declined to transfer his services to the purchasers, and returned by an overland journey to Montreal. The party making this journey ascended the Columbia to the great bend, and crossed the mountains to follow the River Athabasca, and the now well-known route to Lake Superior. Leaving Fort George, the new name given to Astoria, on the 4th of April, Franchère and those accompanying him arrived at Montreal on the 1st of September. The original MS. is in the possession of the Public Library, Toronto.

C. Stuart. "The Emigrants' Guide to Upper Canada, or sketches of the present state of that Province, collected from a residence therein during the years 1817, 1818, 1819, interspersed with reflections by C. Stuart, Esq., retired captain of the Honourable the East India Company service, and one of his Majesty's justices of the peace for the western district of Upper Canada. 'Deliberate, Decide and Dare.'" London, 1820. 12mo.

Mr. Stuart formed an unfavourable opinion of the province. He asks the question what was the benefit to be derived by the British government taking steps to defend the country.

Daniel Williams Harmon. "A Journal of Voyages and Travels in the Interior of North America, between the 47th and 58th degrees of north latitude, extending from Montreal nearly to the Pacific Ocean, a distance of near 5,000 miles; including an account of the principal occurrences during a residence of nineteen years in different parts of the country; to which are added a concise description of the face of the country, its inhabitants, their· manners, customs, laws, religion, &c." Andover, 1820. 8vo.

Mr. Harmon left Lachine in 1800 with a party of the North-West Company, and led the life of a fur trader in the region of the Rocky Mountains until 1819, when he returned to Montreal. He was engaged at many of the stations on the Fraser and at Peace River, having lived eight and a half years west of the Rocky Mountains. His work is valuable in many respects, throwing much light on those days, especially from his experience of Indian life.

"A few plain directions for persons intending to proceed as settlers to His Majesty's province of Upper Canada, in North America. Pointing out the best Port to embark at for Quebec. Provisions and other things necessary to be provided for the Voyage," &c., &c., &c. By an English farmer settled in Upper Canada. London, 1820. 12mo.

The advice given in these pages to emigrants is still applicable, although the conditions described are changed. Much that is said holds good for the traveller; for instance, he is warned to look after his baggage. The "farmer" tells us, "a small trunk or other light article may easily be taken away by another passenger *through mistake.*" The taverns of the localities are also described. One matter for surprise is the high fees exacted on the issue of patents for land, a table of which he gives. There is much information concerning the wild animals, the forest trees, and the farm produce of the province. The book is naturally written and was of use in the condition of the country.

J. Strachan. "A Visit to the Province of Upper Canada in 1819." Aberdeen, 1820. 8vo.

The author, the brother of the still well remembered Bishop of Toronto, visited the province in 1819. Having been separated from his brother for more than twenty-five years, the main object of sailing from Aberdeen was once more to see him. He describes the country, its advantages, its geography, the cost of living. As he had had the opportunity of meeting many distinguished persons, he relates some of the conversations held with them, throwing light on several points in dispute. Among other matters he alludes to Mr. Gourlay's career. Some of the stories told are full of humour.

A. Amos. "Report of trials in the Courts of Canada, relative to the destruction of the Earl of Selkirk's settlement on the Red River; with observations." London, 1820. pp. iv. and 388. 8vo.

We have in these pages reports of the trials of the parties implicated in the outrages committed on Lord Selkirk's settlement. Four persons were tried in Montreal in May, 1818, before Chief-Justice Monk and Judge Bowen. Two others were tried at Toronto in October, 1818, before a full bench, for the murder of Governor Semple on the 17th of June, 1816, at the well-known encounter at Seven Oaks. Other parties were included in the arraignment, but they did not appear. They were all found "not guilty." These trials, with three others of the same character, are reported in full, the object of the publication of the book being, it is said, to illustrate the administration of justice in Canada, with regard to the North-West; the greatest criminals escaping all legal consequence of their misdeeds, from the protection of the North-West Company.

There are a great many publications extant, which were written at this time, on the rival claims of the North-West and Hudson's Bay Companies; some of a few pages, in other cases they present a good sized volume. For a time the antagonistic pretensions of these two bodies were advocated with much acrimony. It is not possible in this calendar to enter into the circumstances of this old quarrel, the result of which has passed out of memory with the events which characterized it. The history is to be sought in many narratives, written in much bitterness of spirit, many of the writers having been prominent actors in the dispute.

I do not conceive it to be a part of my duty to re-integrate these forgotten volumes. The events which they record are only of local interest, and do not bear upon the history of Canada of that period.

D. Dainville. "Beautés de l'histoire du Canada ou Epoques mémorables, traits intéressants, mœurs, usages, coutumes des Habitans du Canada, tant indigènes que Colons, depuis sa découverte jusqu'à ce jour." Paris, 1821. 12mo.

The author of this work it is believed was Mr. Gustave Bossange, of the firm of the well-known booksellers at Paris. In a familiar

E

style he relates the first voyages of discovery, and the settlement and early years of Quebec, with a compressed narrative of the history of the country to the date of publication. In the same form he describes the manners and customs of the Indians.

This volume would still be useful to any one knowing nothing of the subject, desirous of rapidly gaining some information regarding it ; provided he did not look for critical accuracy of the facts presented. The seventy years which have elapsed since its appearance have much modified many of the opinions expressed. The book, however, is simply and naturally written, and may be taken as a model for a work of a similar character.

C. Smart. " The Emigrant's guide to Upper Canada : or Sketches of the present State of that Province, collected from a residence therein during the years 1817, 1818, 1819. Interspersed with reflections." London, 1821. pp. 335. 12mo.

I have not been able to meet this volume.

Henry J. Finn. "Montgomery; or, the Falls of Montmorenci. A new national drama." Boston, 1821.

The author, an actor, made his first appearance in Montreal in 1811.

John Howison. "Sketches of Upper Canada, Domestic, Local and Characteristic : to which are added Practical Details for the information of Emigrants of every class, and some Recollections of the United States." Edinburg, 1821. 8vo.

The writer of this volume travelled from Quebec through Canada to Sandwich, where he crossed the Detroit River to pass into the United States. We do not meet with any profound observations, but the author is always sensible, and, not writing for effect, generally expresses himself with fairness and accuracy. He formed definite views from what he experienced, and points out, that to those desirous of being exempt from the restrictions of fashion and ceremony, with small incomes and moderate expectations, Canada could not fail to be an agreeable place of residence.

Wm. Dalton. "Travels in the United States of America and part of Upper Canada." Appleby, 1821. 12mo.

This traveller crossed the river Niagara at Fort Erie and reached Queenston, whence he passed over to Lewiston. It was the only "part of Upper Canada" visited by him.

Robert Lamond, Secretary and Agent. "A narrative of the rise and progress of emigration from the counties of Lanark and Renfrew to the new settlements in Upper Canada, in government grant, comprising the proceedings of the Glasgow Committee, for directing the affairs and embarkation of the Societies; with a map of the Townships, Designs for Cottages and a Plan of the Ship 'Earl of Buckinghamshire,' also interesting letters from the settlements." Glasgow, 1821. 8vo.

This is a brief account of the emigration which took place in 1820-21, from the western counties of Scotland to the Perth or Bathurst districts of Upper Canada. Subscriptions were obtained to assist those emigrating, and committees were formed, so that those leaving their homes might do so on conditions as favourable as possible.

P. Stansbury. "A Pedestrian Tour of 2,300 miles in North America, to the Lakes, the Canadas and the New England States, performed in the autumn of 1821 (with engravings)." New York, 1822. 12mo.

The writer, a citizen of the United States, frequently introduces historical narrative, written from his own national standing-point. It is not a work to repay perusal.

Robert Fleming Gourlay. "General Introduction to Statistical Account of Upper Canada, compiled with a view to a grand system of Emigration, in connexion with a reform of the poor Laws." London, 1822. 8vo.

"Statistical Account of Upper Canada (with Maps)." 2 vols. London, 1822.

It will be seen by this calendar that Mr. Gourlay commenced the publication of pamphlets as early as 1818. The above work did not appear until four years later. His name will be preserved on account of the cruel treatment he received; he was imprisoned as an alien, and as a seditious person brought within the meaning of the statute of 1804. When it is remembered that Mr. Gourlay was a Scotchman by birth, this painful proceeding would appear almost impossible. A writ of *habeas corpus* was granted, but bail was refused. Gourlay accordingly remained in Niagara jail, where he was treated with great harshness. He was finally tried for refusing to obey an order to leave the province. He was found guilty, and forced to take his departure ; by the way of the United States he reached England. The event took place in the administration of Sir Peregrine Maitland. The act, however, in no way affected his position as lieutenant-governor, for he remained in Canada until 1828. How history will judge the proceeding is another matter.

John McDonald. " Narrative of a voyage to Quebec, and journey from thence to New Lanark in Upper Canada, detailing the hardships and difficulties which an emigrant has to encounter, before and after his settlement ; with an account of the country as regards its climate, soil and the actual condition of its inhabitants." Glasgow, 1822. 8vo.

The writer, as one may conceive by the title, does not give a cheerful view of an emigrant's life. He reached Prescott, where he remained three weeks, and then proceeded on his journey. He left the Saint Lawrence at Brockville, and reached Perth ; and started for New Lanark, fourteen miles distant. In his journey McDonald broke one of his ribs. Entertaining extremely religious views, he was frequently pained at the somewhat free life of the settlers. The circulation of many works of this character would not have been a great encouragement to emigration.

John William Bannister. " Sketches of plans for settling in Upper Canada a portion of the Unemployed Labourers of Great Britain and Ireland." By a settler. London, 1821. 8vo. 2nd Ed., 1822. 3rd Ed., 1826.

The object to be attained in the view of the writer was the settlement of the country by such as were indigent, in which the province should assist.  One of his schemes was that the cost of the voyage to Canada should be borne by the mother country, that the province should construct what is now known as the Trent river canal, and that 6,000 immigrants, men, women and children, should be established in the neighbourhood of the works at government expense. The subject of the Indians of Upper Canada also received attention. Another work of this writer, "Emigration to Canada," 1831, 8vo., is the same book with some additional remarks as to Nova Scotia.

John M. Duncan.  "Travels through part of the United States and Canada, 1818 and 1819."  Glasgow, 1823.  2 vols., 8vo.

Mr. Duncan entered Canada from Black Rock, near Buffalo. After visiting the falls he descended the Saint Lawrence to Montreal and Quebec, and after a stay of two months, October and November, he continued his journey in the United States.  His observations are those of the tourist who feels that he has something to say.  To-day they have little interest.

H. Wilson.  "The Wanderer in America, or Truth at Home ; comprising a statement of observations and facts relative to the United States and Canada, North America ; the result of an Extensive Personal Tour, and from Sources of Information the most Authentic; including soil, climate, manners, and customs, of civilized inhabitants and Indians, anecdotes, &c., of distinguished characters."

> " I will a round, unvarnished tale deliver."
> "      *      *      nothing extenuate
> " Or set down aught in malice.
>
> SHAKESPEARE.

Thirsk, 1823.  6s.

The volume contains a dedication to Lord Dalhousie, dated Quebec, 1821.  Mr. Wilson landed at New York, on which city he makes his comments, and passed by Albany to Sackett's Harbour, Lake Ontario, where he took the steamboat for York [Toronto]. He extended his journey to Amherstburg, and revisiting York, he descended the Saint Lawrence to Montreal. After a short stay in the city he returned by the way of Lake Champlain to the States.

On leaving Canada, Mr. Wilson remarks, "I cannot but wonder why England retains so unprofitable an appendage to her dominions, the only answer there can be made will bear an analogy with Montreal feeling, that is, *Timber*. One-half is boundless snow, and the other half literally a wilderness ; it is a colony maintained at enormous expence" [p. 62]. This strongly expressed view, with two strophes to the " Memory of Tecumseh," beginning

" Tecumseh has no grave, but eagles dipt
     Their ravening beaks, and drank his stout heart's tide,"

formed Mr. Wilson's valedictory to Canada.

There is much criticism on matters having little relation one with the other. It would be difficult to explain the author's reasons for the publication of the volume, except by the unfortunate universal failing of humanity : vanity.

Rev. William Bell. "Hints to Emigrants ; in a series of letters from Upper Canada. Illustrated with a map and plans." Edinburgh, 1824. 236pp. 12mo.

The author, a minister of the Church of Scotland, in 1812, in consequence of a petition to the Presbytery of Edinburgh, was appointed minister of Perth, north of Brockville, in the then district of Bathurst, and sent out with his family to Canada. He explains, that the book, which consists of a series of letters, was published to give information to emigrants, especially to those designing to reach Perth and the northern settlements at Lanark, lately commenced. The consequence is, that we meet more in this volume concerning this district, than in other similar publications of the date. As a rule, attention was generally given to the route by the Saint Lawrence to Toronto, and to those proceeding west and north of that place. Mr. Bell dwelt forcibly on the fact that many believed when they arrived at Quebec, their difficulties were over ; whereas, having landed, the expence of reaching their destination in other parts of the province was as great as the cost of the sea voyage. He describes naturally and pleasantly his passage to Quebec, and his steamboat journey to Montreal, which took some thirty-six hours. Mr. Bell tells us that some rollicking

" bucks," as he calls them, were on board, who caroused to a late
hour, when one of them went round to the passengers' berths,
awakening their occupants and asking them if they had seen some
mythical personage. Those who conceived the joke were uproari-
ously merry over it. Afterwards, they diversified the entertain-
ment by dog-howls, cat-calls, and the singing of a hymn, learned,
as the performer declared, at a methodist meeting. Everything
must come to an end, so these individuals retired, not creating on
Mr. Bell's mind a "favourable impression" "of the manners of
Canadian gentlemen."

Mr. Bell ascended the Saint Lawrence in a *bateau*. He left
Lachine on the 12th of June, and reached Prescott on the 18th. A
graphic account is given of his journey, extending over some pages
[49-60] ; as a picture of the mode of travelling of the time, it could
be profitably reprinted.

From Prescott Mr. Bell crossed by waggon to Perth, passing by
Brockville. He had his difficulties with his new parishioners ; on
this point the volume must be consulted. He gives a carefully
written description of Canada as he saw it, and he enters into much
which then happened, never, however, forgetting that he is a
minister of his church. Thus, he tells us [p. 297], "Sir Peregrine
Maitland, the present Lieutenant-Governor of the province of
Upper Canada, is a decided friend to religion. Every Sabbath day,
whether at home or abroad, he attends public worship twice if he
has it in his power, and always conducts himself in the church with
the greatest reverence and propriety. Would to God that all great
men would imitate his example." His wife, the Lady Sarah
Maitland, she was the daughter of the duke of Richmond, with
whom Maitland, one of the handsomest men of his time, after
Waterloo ran away with, is equally commended, "the Sunday
schools . . in particular engaged her attention." A devotional
spirit runs through the work, but it is restrained by sound sense.
The work is in every respect readable, and it is particularly worthy
the attention of the local investigator, for he will find many facts
he can embody in his narrative.

Messrs. Sewell, Stuart, Robinson and Strachan. " Plan
for a General Legislative Union of the British Provinces in
North America." London, 1824. 8vo.

[Attributed to Captain Blaney]. "An Excursion through
the United States and Canada, during the years 1822–23.
By an English gentleman." London, 1824. 8vo.

We can read here the remarks of an educated gentleman, whose
object in visiting the United States was to pass his time pleasantly,
and to obtain information. Very few pages are given to Canada.
He descended the Saint Lawrence from Niagara to Montreal, and
returned to New York by Lake Champlain. The Saint Lawrence
he described as by far "the most beautiful river he had ever
seen." His preference, however, was given to the State of New
York, as he considered Canada to be without enterprise; although
he was one of the earliest writers who did justice to the climate of
the province. That of Upper Canada he considered as particularly
fine. On the 6th of June he found the heat of the sun at Niagara
almost insupportable, and on that day he saw two hundred hum-
ming birds on the Canadian side of the river.

The volume, although pleasantly written, is of no value for
reference.

Adam Hodgson. "Letters from North America, written
during a Tour in the United States and Canada." London,
1824. 2 vols., 8vo.

These volumes are principally confined to the journey in the
United States. In 1822 a flying visit was made to Montreal and
Quebec. Mr. Hodgson left Canada by Lake Champlain. His visit
included only a few days at the end of August and the commencement of September.

Lieut. J. C. Morgan, Royal Marines. "The Emigrant's
Note Book and Guide; with Recollections of Upper and
Lower Canada during the late War." London, 1824. 12mo.

Mr. Morgan was a lieutenant in the second battalion of the Royal
Marines, and served in the war. He was then on half-pay. He
writes from the standing-point of a British officer with regard to
Canada. The volume contains a view of the Chaudière Falls, near
Quebec, drawn on stone by Harding.

Edward Allen Talbot. "Five years' residence in the

Canadas, including a Tour through part of the United States of America in the year 1823." London, 1824. 2 vols., 8vo. Translated by M. Eries. Paris, 1825. 3 vols., 8vo.

This Edward Talbot must not be confounded with the Hon. Thomas Talbot, of the 24th regiment, who came to Upper Canada in 1790 as private secretary to Governor Simcoe, the founder of the Talbot settlement, and who died in February, 1853. Mr. Talbot's work is a record of his experience, and is still a readable book. After a general examination of the province with his family, he finally established himself in the Talbot district. He gives much general information on many points. He observed with care the habits of the wild animals and birds of the country, and collected many facts concerning them, when to do so was more easy of attainment than at present. He not only gave his attention to the beasts, birds and insects, but also correctly described the forest, and fruit-bearing trees, with the vegetables which could be produced. His observations extend to the condition of morality and religion. At the same time, he endeavours to furnish a picture of the social state of Canada embracing every condition; he likewise comments upon the political institutions and the courts of law. Indeed, it may be said that there is scarcely a subject which he has left untouched; he always leads to the belief that he has written carefully and conscientiously.

"A short sketch of the Province of Upper Canada, for the information of the labouring poor throughout England, &c., &c. By Henry John Boulton, &c., &c., His Majesty's Solicitor-General for the Province of Upper Canada." London, 1826. 12mo.

This work, which is a pamphlet in favour of emigration, is only included in this list owing to Mr. Boulton having been at this date Solicitor-General of Upper Canada. His object in publishing the volume was, as he puts it, "to afford information to the lower classes." It calls for no especial remark.

Bishop Strachan. "Remarks on emigration from the United Kingdom. By John Strachan, D.D., Archdeacon of York, Upper Canada; addressed to Robert Wilmot Horton,

Esq., M.P., Chairman of the Select Committee of Emigration in the last Parliament." London, 1827. 8vo.

The author of this work is best remembered as Bishop of Toronto, to which dignity he was nominated in 1839. The work is in favour of emigration to Canada, as extending relief to the redundant population of the mother country ; on the ground that the colonies offered " good neighbourhood, health, independence and even opulence." After describing Upper and Lower Canada, the bishop sets forth his scheme of government emigration, viz. : that 750,000 persons should be sent at the expense of the state ; men, women and children, 150,000 families. From Ireland, 100,000 ; England, 40,000 ; Scotland, 10,000 ; at the rate of 15,000 families annually. The cost annually would be one million and a half pounds, to be divided, one million as the charge of Ireland, and half a million of England and Scotland ; the money to be borrowed and to be repaid by a rate on land and houses ; after the seventh year of settlement the emigrants to pay an assessment towards repayment of the expenditure. The author's calculation was that at the end of seventeen years the debt would be extinguished. It was one of the many schemes proposed, somewhat discussed, and soon to be forgotten. In the "Memoir" of Bishop Strachan [Bishop Bethune ; Rowsell, Toronto, 1870], p. 117, a letter, 29th January, 1827, is given, in which the bishop relates. that he has written a pamphlet on "Emigration" of nearly 100 pages, and "an appeal of 24 pages in favour of our College ;" also that he had nearly finished an abridgement of the Emigration Report of the Committee of the House of Commons, undertaken at the request of the under-secretary for the colonies, Mr. Wilmot Horton. The reward he hoped for, was the charter of the university.

Thomas Johnston. "Travels through Lower Canada, interspersed with Canadian tales and anecdotes, and interesting information to intending emigrants." Edinburgh, 1827. 12mo.

I have not seen this book.

Hon. Frederick Fitzgerald De Roos, Lieut. R.N. " Personal Narrative of Travels in the United States and Canada

in 1826, with remarks on the present state of the American
Navy (with plates)." 1827. 8vo.

Lieutenant de Roos arrived at Quebec in H.M.S. "Jupiter." He
ascended the Saint Lawrence to Niagara, where, after passing some
pleasant hours, he returned to his starting point. His visit to the
United States led him to form the opinion that the naval strength
of the country had been exaggerated.

A. C. Buchanan, Emigration Agent, Quebec. "Emigration practically considered, with detailed directions to Emigrants proceeding to British North America." London,
1828. 8vo.

A second edition was brought out in 1834. Mr. Buchanan held
the position of Emigration Agent for many years, until his death
in 1869.

P. Finan. "Journal of a voyage to Quebec in the year
1825, with recollections of Canada during the late American
War in the years 1812, 1813." Newry, 1828. 12mo.

The writer left Newry in Ireland for Quebec. The first hundred
pages, one-fourth of the volume, are devoted to the account of his
voyage. The country is described as he saw it, but there is nothing
in this respect to invite reference to the book. The second part
contains the writer's experience in 1812, 1813. He was with his
father, an officer of a regiment, apparently the 8th, and was
present on the 27th of April, 1813, when Toronto was burned by
the United States troops. Finan was an eye-witness of the fact.
He relates an incident I do not remember to have seen elsewhere.
(pp. 286, 287). "While this part of our force was contending with
the enemy in the woods, an unfortunate accident occurred in the
battery opposite to the fleet, which proved a death-blow to the
little hope that might have been entertained of a successful issue to
the proceedings of the day. A gun was aimed at one of the vessels,
and the officers, desirous of seeing if the ball would take effect,
ascended the bastion : in the meantime, the artillery-man, waiting
for the word of command to fire, held the match behind him, as is
usual under such circumstances; and the travelling magazine, a

large wooden chest, containing cartridges for the great guns, being open just at his back, he unfortunately put the match into it, and the consequence, as may be supposed, was dreadful indeed! Every man in the battery was blown into the air, and the *dissection* of the greater part of their bodies was inconceivably shocking! The officers were thrown from the bastion by the shock, but escaped with a few bruises: the cannons were dismounted, and, consequently, the battery was rendered completely useless.

I was standing at the gate of the garrison when the poor soldiers who escaped the explosion with a little life remaining were brought into the hospital, and a more afflicting sight could scarcely be witnessed. Their faces were completely black, resembling those of the blackest Africans; their hair frizzled like theirs, and their clothes scorched and emitting an effluvia so strong as to be perceived long before they reached one. One man in particular presented an awful spectacle: he was brought in a wheelbarrow, and from his appearance I should be inclined to suppose that almost every bone in his body was broken; he was lying in a powerless heap, shaking about with every motion of the barrow, from which his legs hung dangling down, as if only connected with his body by the skin, while his cries and groans were of the most heart-rending description."

He also describes the shooting of a deserter, at which he was present.

John Mactaggart. "Three years in Canada: an account of the actual state of the country in 1826-7-8, comprehending its resources, productions, improvements and capabilities; and including Sketches of the state of society, advice to Emigrants, &c." London, 1829. 2 vols., 8vo.

Mr. John Mactaggart was selected by the celebrated engineer Rennie, when requested by the British government to recommend a clerk of the works for the Rideau Canal. In 1828 he returned to England, suffering from "the malaria of the swampy wastes," when he published his reminiscences in two volumes. He gives much information concerning this line of navigation.

Hugh Murray, F.R.S.E. "Historical account of Discoveries and Travels in North America; including the United States, Canada, the Shores of the Polar Sea, and the Voyages

in search of a North-West Passage; with Observations on
Emigration; illustrated by a Map of North America."
London, 1829. 2 vols., 8vo.

The author has brought together much information on the subject
of the early discoveries on the American continent. He includes
what he could learn regarding Canada. The book shews industry
and research.

Captain Basil Hall. "Travels in North America in the
years 1827 and 1828." Edinburgh, 1829. 3 vols., 8vo.

Captain Hall crossed into Canada from Niagara, visited the
Grand River, the Otonabee, and stopping at several towns in his
descent of the Saint Lawrence, finally reached Montreal and
Quebec. His remarks are those of a well educated man of the
world. At the time of its publication the book attracted attention;
little is to be learned by reference to it sixty-five years after it was
written.

Captain Basil Hall. "Forty Etchings from Sketches
made with the Camera-Lucida in North America in 1827
and 1829." Edinburg, 1829.

The volume contains ten views of Canada: Niagara, Peter-
borough, the Saint Lawrence, &c., &c.

"A political and historical account of Lower Canada;
with remarks on the present situation of the people as
regards their manners, character, religion." By a "Canadian." London, 1830. 8vo.

The work, originally written in French, was translated for publication in London, and is attributed to Dr. Pierre Salles de la
Terrière. It was professedly in answer to a book published in
Montreal, under the title of "Political Annals of Lower Canada,
being a review of the Political and Legislative history of that
province." By a British settler.

The writer gives a brief history of the province from his point of
view to the date at which he wrote. He dwelt upon the misunder-
standing which had long existed between the Canadian Government

and the House of Assembly, which had increased in intensity under the governorship of Lord Dalhousie. The remedy proposed by him was the abolition of the Legislative Council.

Several important public documents are included in the appendix, some of which are only imperfectly known.

William Cattermole. "The advantages of Emigration to Canada, being the substance of Two Lectures delivered at the Town-hall, Colchester, and the Mechanics' Institution, Ipswich." London, May, 1831. 12mo.

The object of this volume was to advocate emigration to Canada in preference to the United States. It describes the province, with its geography, climate, soil and productions; likewise giving an account of the principal towns. A history of the Canada Company also is added. The book contained information of value when published, which, doubtless, had its good effect on those hesitating as to their future career. At this date it furnishes the modern writer some important facts, to aid in shewing the condition of the province when Mr. Cattermole wrote.

Josiah Conder. "United States and Canada," London, 1831. 12mo.

Only a slight space is allotted to Canada. What is there said is evidently taken from works previously published.

Ross Cox. "Adventures on the Columbia River, including the Narrative of a Residence of six years on the western side of the Rocky Mountains, among various Tribes of Indians hitherto unknown, together with a journey across the American Continent." London, 1831. 2 vols., 8vo. New York, 1832.

Mr. Cox was one of the party who proceeded to Astoria with Mr. Astor. On the retirement of the Pacific Fur Company he joined the new association. He remained in the service until 1817, when he returned by an overland journey to Montreal, which he reached in September.

Martin Doyle. "Hints on Emigration to Upper Canada,

especially addressed to the middle and lower classes in Great Britain and Ireland." Dublin, London, Edinburg, 1831.

Mr. Doyle was a voluminous writer on agricultural subjects. He was the author of a cyclopædia of practical husbandry and rural affairs, published in 1829 [2nd Ed. enlarged in 1851]. He did much to improve the condition of the labouring classes in Ireland, and urged in various publications and through the daily press the importance of what he called "cottage farming." The above work advocates emigration, to use his own words, as "a prudent remedy" for a large class of the population.

George Henry Hume. "Canada as it is, comprising details relating to the Domestic Policy, Commerce and Agriculture of the Upper and Lower Provinces, comprising matter of general information and interest, especially intended for the use of settlers and emigrants," New York, 1832. 12mo.

Although this work bears the imprint of a New York publisher [Stodart, Courtland Street], and has no reference to Canada on the title page, there is internal evidence that it was written in the province, probably in Upper Canada. It is not mentioned either in Lowndes or Allibone. It is put together with some care from the standing-point of desiring to see a large emigration directed to Canada, so that the province might become prosperous and wealthy. In the preface we meet the suggestive sentence that a "neighboring power has already cast a jealous eye on this northern territory." It is one of the best books of the class, and contains much sound information. The concluding pages are given to a description of the birds. While there is an absence of political partisanship, many of the events of the time are narrated, and the prominent towns are described with some fullness. The volume also furnishes a more extended account of the valley of the Ottawa than is generally found at that date. This unpretending book will repay reference to it, especially on the subject of the tillage of the land, to which the writer had evidently given careful attention.

Robert Mudie. "The Emigrant's Pocket Companion; containing : what emigration is, who should be emigrants, where emigrants should go ; a description of British North

America, especially the Canadas, and full instructions to intending emigrants." London, 1832.

Mr. Mudie commences at the starting point by stating what emigration is, and who should be emigrants. He saw that a British subject was an alien in the United States, and he felt ground of objection against Western and Southern Africa, and Australia. His preference was declared for British North America. He describes in a few pages Newfoundland, Nova Scotia, New Brunswick and Upper and Lower Canada. He gathered together much that was new, and gave some excellent advice. Sixty years ago there was requirement for this special information. Even to-day its constant dissemination is considered necessary, and has become a matter of government care. The object of the writer, as he expresses it, was "to clear away some of the mist that has been suffered to gather, or which has probably in some cases been intuitively gathered around the question of emigration."

Andrew Picken. "The Canadas as they at present commend themselves to the enterprise of Emigrants, Colonists and Capitalists, comprehending a variety of Topographical Reports concerning the quality of the land, &c., in different Districts; and the fullest general information: compiled and condensed from original documents furnished by John Galt, Esquire, and other authentic sources; with a map." London, Wilson, 1832. 1 vol,, 8vo.

This work is apparently a compilation in the interest of the American Land Company and the Canada Land Company to encourage emigration. Several official documents are published, with many papers and reports, of value for reference at the time. The book contains much local information, useful to a class of writers occupied in the preservation of the history of certain districts.

Joseph Pickering, late of Penny Stratford, Berks., and now of Canada. "Inquiries of an Emigrant; being the narrative of an English farmer from the year 1824 to 1830, during which he traversed the United States and Canada,

with a view to settle as an Emigrant, containing observations
on the manners, soil, climate and husbandry of the Americans;
estimates of outfit, charges of voyage and travelling
expenses." London, 1832. Small 8vo.

The writer was engaged as an overseer on Col. Talbot's farm.
He remained in this position for some time, and visited the province
with the view of obtaining the information which he embodied in
the volume.

John M'Gregor. " British America." 2 vols., 8vo.
Edinburgh and London, 1832.

The first volume refers to Newfoundland, Prince Edward island,
and the Maritime Provinces. Book VII. of the second volume
relates to Lower Canada. Book VIII. to Upper Canada.
A history of British America is given as it was written sixty
years ago, being brought down to date to the governorship of Lord
Aylmer. The book is a careful compendium of all that had
appeared to that time. The volume therefore narrates many events
and incidents of a varied character, accompanied by much local
description, and throughout is pleasant reading. Mr. M'Gregor
can, however, scarcely be considered an authority. He covers a
great deal of ground, and furnishes his readers with a great many
facts, undoubtedly carefully gathered, likewise with many statistical notes. For general information few books were at the date
more useful, for the author was industrious and intelligent. A
careful inquirer, nevertheless, in referring to these volumes will
find it necessary to consult original authorities on much which
is stated in them.

" The Canadas as they now are, comprehending a view of
their climate, rivers, lakes, canals, government, laws, taxes,
towns, trade, &c., with a description of the soil and advantages or disadvantages of every township in the province,"
&c., &c. By a late resident. London, 1833.

It is claimed that this book is written concisely, with the view of
giving information to the emigrant, and it aspires to no higher
pretension than simply and naturally to narrate the author's views

F

of the country. At the time much which is related was new to many in the old country; perhaps in some quarters there is no great improvement in this respect. But avowedly written to aid emigration at that date, the volume presupposes an entire want of knowledge on the part of his readers.

Francis A. Evans. "The Emigrants' Directory and Guide to obtain lands and effect a settlement in the Canadas." 1833. 12mo.

Mr. Evans came to Canada in 1813, and obtained some land near Drummondville, on the Saint Francis River, in the Eastern Townships. In 1824 he was appointed government land agent. The townships obtained representation in the legislature of 1829. [11th March]. On the bill being sanctioned at home, eight members were returned without waiting for the general election, and the parliament which met on the 22nd January, 1830, for the first time received two members each for Mississquoi, Sherbrooke and Stanstead, and one member each for Shefford and Drummond, making a total of eight members, Mr. Evans took his seat as a member on this occasion. It is melancholy to record, that between the date when the "advertisement" was written in 1832, and the appearance of the volume in 1833, Mr. Evans died from cholera, after a few hours' illness.

The work contains much information regarding the early settlement of the Eastern Townships. We are made to feel that the author, after his own observation, formed the opinions which he sets forth with much good sense,

William Gourlay. "A guide to the Canadas, containing useful and practical information for those who propose emigrating to the British possessions in North America." By William Gourlay, late merchant in Ayr, who has just returned from the Canadas, where he has resided for a number of years. Ayr, 1833. Small 8vo.

Mr. William Gourlay must not be confounded with Mr. Robert Fleming Gourlay, whose imprisonment forms so painful a passage in the political history of the country. The author tells us that though bred a farmer he was induced to become a mechanic, and eventually started as an ironmonger, which business he followed for twenty years. In consequence of unfortunate speculations he tried his fortunes in Canada, where he remained for some years, when, owing to family affairs, he returned to his native place.

The work is not without information, and is sensibly written. Much is said in regard to prices and the cost of living.

Stephen Davis. "Notes of a tour in America in 1832 and 1833." By Stephen Davis, Collecting Agent of the Baptist Society for Ireland. Edinburgh, 1833. 12mo.

Mr. Davis landed in New York, and in his tour was induced to visit Montreal by lake Champlain. During the time he was in the city, the Masonic Hall, or British American Hotel, in St. Paul Street, was burnt, in April, 1833. He was preaching when the fire became visible to those in the church; "not more than one or two individuals left the place until the service was concluded." He describes the contrast in the United States. He says: "Upon one occasion, though the fire was at a considerable distance, the place became so deserted, and the agitation of those who lingered so manifest, that I was obliged to break off the discourse entirely." From Montreal Mr. Davis proceeded to Rochester. He also visited Niagara.

T. Sockett. "A letter to a member of parliament, containing a statement of the method pursued by the Petworth Committee, on sending out emigrants to Upper Canada, in the years 1832 and 1833, and a plan upon which the sums required for defraying the expence of emigration may be raised." London, 1833. Large 8vo.

This is an account of the system adopted in sending out emigrants from the neighbourhood of Petworth in 1832. Lord Egremont having stated his willingness to afford liberal assistance to artisans and labourers living on his estate and in the neighbourhood desirous of emigrating, a Committee was formed to carry out the purpose. For the protection of the emigrants, an agent was engaged, whose duty it was to conduct the party to Toronto, and to have regard to their destination and well-being. At Toronto they were seen by the Lieut.-Governor, and forwarded to the localities assigned them, and care was taken, as far as possible, to provide for the future.

Lord Egremont paid the whole passage-money for those leaving Petworth and the four adjoining parishes. The outfit was supplied from the poor rate. The arrangement for the comfort and protection of the passengers was in the highest degree satisfactory. Several letters are appended, recording the well-doing of the writers.

" Letters from Sussex Emigrants who sailed from Portsmouth in April, 1832, on board the ships 'Lord Melville' and ' Eveline,' for Upper Canada," &c., &c. 8vo. 1833.

These letters even now can be read with interest, but at the date of their publication they must have exercised some influence on those struggling in difficulty, who by emigration were desirous of bettering their fortunes. Much miscellaneous information is added for the use of those entertaining the intention.

William Lyon Mackenzie. " Sketches of Canada and the United States." London, 1833. 8vo.

The book is described by Mr. Lindsey as "treating of a great variety of subjects, having no connection and without arrangement." It really consists of notes taken during travels in Canada and the United States. There is, however, "an agreeable seasoning of racy and remarkable anecdotes."

Captain J. E. Alexander, 42nd Royal Highlanders. " Transatlantic Sketches, comprising visits to the most interesting scenes in North and South America and the West Indies, with Notes on Negro Slavery and Canadian Emigration." 2 vols. London, 1833. Philadelphia, 1833. 8vo.

Captain, afterwards Sir, James Alexander in his Canadian travels crossed the Niagara River, and landed at Chippewa. He wandered some days about Niagara Falls, which he describes. At York (Toronto) he met Sir John Colborne, and at his invitation was present at the river Credit, when Colonel Givings gave the annual presents to the Mississaga Indians. At Kingston he made inquiries as to the Rideau Canal. He descended the Saint Lawrence, and, sleeping a night at the Cascades, ascended the Ottawa to Bytown. With Colonel By, Captain Alexander followed the Rideau to Jones' Falls. Although a description is given of the further route of this navigation, it does not appear that the traveller went beyond this point. Captain Alexander visited Montreal and Quebec, and relates some pleasant recollections of the *personnel* of that day. Even to recording the absurd speech of the then Governor-General, Lord Aylmer : "As I set about my daily task of duty, it teaches me to ask myself this question, ' What can I do this day to promote the happiness and prosperity of Canada ! ' "

Rev. Isaac Fidler. "Observations on Professions, Literature, Manners and Emigration in the United States and Canada, made during a residence in 1832." London, 1833. 12mo. Reprinted, New York, 1833. 18mo.

The author left England in 1831 for the United States. Finally, he determined to seek his fortunes in Canada. In 1833 he published his volume in London. Crossing to Niagara he proceeded thence to Quebec, to obtain a position in the Colonial Church. He there saw Bishop Stewart, who offered to appoint him to Newmarket, his labours extending to Penetanguishene. There is an expression of the Bishop's worthy of record. Fidler did not consider himself "equal to such journeys as the mission exacted." " I myself," replied his lordship, "have performed much greater journeys than the one proposed to you, on foot and unattended. I was a missionary for thirty-five years, at a period when the country was in a less civilized state, and when greater self-denial than is required of you was unavoidably imposed on the preachers of the gospel. There is no part of my large diocese which I have not visited and travelled on foot, with a Bible my sole companion and only solace. What, therefore, is proferred for your acceptance is not to be compared in labours and privations to what has been experienced before you." Mr. Fidler was offered the mission at Thornhill, 14 miles from Toronto, which he accepted ; he shortly returned to England. Mr. Fidler expresses the views he formed when in Canada : as might be expected, allusions to the position of a clergyman are frequently to be met.

I. Finch. " Travels in the United States of America and

Canada, containing some account of their scientific institutions, &c., &c." London, 1833. 8vo.

Only a few pages of this work are given to Canada. They are without importance.

T. W. Magrath. "Authentic letters from Upper Canada, with an account of Canadian Field Sports." The Etchings by Samuel Lover. Edited by the Rev. T. Radcliff. Dublin, 1833. 12mo.

This work brings to view the experience of a settler in 1831, with cost of establishment in Canada. It consists of letters written familiarly by the author to a friend in Ireland. Much is said of the life of the sportsmen of the date.

Lieut. E. T. Coke. "A Subaltern's Furlough; descriptive Scenes in various parts of the United States, Upper and Lower Canada, New Brunswick and Nova Scotia, during the summer and autumn of 1832." Maps and Illustrations. London, 1833. New York, 1833. 12mo.

The author visited the United States, and crossed to Canada from Black Rock. He descended the Saint Lawrence, and from Quebec passed over the Temiscouata Portage to reach the Saint John, which he followed to Fredericton.

On the 6th of September, with two guides, Mr. Coke left Kamouraska. Following the Saint Lawrence for nine miles, the small party turned southward and lost sight of the great river. Several log huts were seen on the route; on the first night the travellers were refused admission for a night's rest. The last application for shelter was, however, successful, and the old couple who received them could with difficulty, next morning, be persuaded to accept any acknowledgment of their hospitality. Here the road in its good sense ceased; there was only a rough trail to follow. From time to time the travellers had to cut their way through windfalls, and the cart often sunk to the axle in the soft places. They were greatly troubled with flies. The following night they reached the farm of Mr. Frazer, described as the Seigneur of Rivière du Loup, who gave them house-room and furnished them with canoes. From the

Temiscouata lake they descended the Madawaska river, portaging to escape the falls, and reached the settlement of Madawaska at the confluence of the Saint John, which they descended to Fredericton. What is specially to be remarked in this volume is the admirable drawing of Mr. Coke. Few better views of the Falls have ever been given, certainly not in a book of this character.

"Statistical Sketches of Upper Canada." By a Backwoodsman. London, 3rd Ed., 1833. 12mo.

This work contains much good advice, which the lately arrived emigrant of modern times could profitably consider. There is a great deal of sound sense in the recommendations made, evidently the result of experience, for the book is dated from Goderich, lake Huron. The author's remarks on field sports may also be profitably read by all fond of that phase of life. Among other things, he tells us, " in hunting the bear, take all the curs in the village along with you. Game dogs are useless for this purpose, for, unless properly trained, they fly at the throat, and get torn to pieces or hugged to death for their pains. The curs yelp after him, bite his rump and make him tree, where he can be shot."

The author was the well-known Dr. William Dunlop, celebrated in Canadian life as "The Tiger." See Galt's Autobiography, vol. II., chap. 9, note.

Adam Fergusson. " Practical Notes made during a tour in Canada and a portion of the United States in 1831, to which are added Notes made during a second visit to Canada in 1833." Edinburgh, 2nd ed., 1834. 8vo.

Mr. Fergusson was born at Woodhill, Perthshire, in 1782, of which county he was a magistrate and Deputy Lieutenant. He was successively a member of the Legislative Council of Upper Canada, and, after the Union of the Provinces, of the Legislative Council of Canada. He died in 1842.

Mr. Fergusson entered Canada by Lake Champlain. He visited Quebec, Montreal, the Falls, and proceeded to York [Toronto]. He met in his travels a Mr. Forsyth, who, on being asked if his family was numerous, " Why," said he " sir, I don't know what you call numerous. *I've raised* nineteen : ten by my first wife, and nine by my second. Mr. Fergusson relates the story of Morgan having been forced over the Falls in 1826 by the Free-Masons as if he believed it. He visited Guelph, Hamilton, and St. Catharines'. What gives his book value is his practical advice to emigrants.

"The United States and Canada in 1832, 1833, and 1834." By C. D. Arfewedson. London, 1834. 2 vols. 8vo.

Only a few unimportant pages of this book apply to Canada.

Tr. Bromme. "Reisen durch die Vereinigten Staaten und Ober Canada." Baltimore, 1834. 3 vols., 8vo.

I have not been able to meet these volumes.

George R. Young. "The British North American Colonies. Letters to the Right Hon. E. G. Stanley, M.P., upon the existing Treaties with France and America, as regard 'Their Rights of Fishery' upon the Coasts of Nova Scotia, Labrador and Newfoundland ; the violations of these Treaties by the subjects of both powers, and their effect upon the commerce, equally of the Mother Country and the Colonies, &c." London, 1834. pp. 193. 8vo. Map.

"The History, Principles and Prospects of the Bank of British North America and of the Colonial Bank ; with an Enquiry into Colonial Exchanges and expediency of introducing British Sterling and British Coin, in preference to the dollar as the money of account and currency of the North American Colonies." Do. 1838. 8vo.

"On the Escheat Question in Prince Edward's Island : Agitation and Remedies." Do. 1838.

"The Canadian Question." Do. 1839.

Letters on "Responsible Government," and an Union of the Colonies of British North America, to the Right Hon. John Russell, Halifax. 1840.

I mention Mr. Young's works owing to the number which bear

his name. They will, however, be more properly described with the pamphlets of the time, than be admitted into this classification.

"Canada in the years 1832, 1833, and 1834, containing important information and instructions to persons intending to emigrate thither in 1835." By an Ex-settler, who resided chiefly "in the bush" for the last two years. Dublin, 1835.

This work is what its name suggests it would be.

"Journal of an excursion to the United States and Canada in the year 1834 ; with hints to emigrants ; and a fair and impartial exposition of the advantages and disadvantages attending emigration by a citizen of Edinburgh." Edinburgh, 1835. 16mo.

The author visited the United States on a tour of pleasure. Landing at New York, he came by steamboat to Albany, by canal boat to Rome, and by stage to Oswego, where he took the steamboat for Toronto, whence he proceeded to Niagara. He pleasantly records his impressions, gathering some anecdotes as he passed onwards. He was not particularly struck with Toronto or Canada. The former he pronounced to be "as dull a hole as I have been in," "with a number of half-pay officers with their noses in red uniform." He further considered it "rather a dissipated place," "wanting that spirit of enterprise you see in the States," the inhabitants reckoning "the importation of emigrants which takes place every spring as their harvest ; and I guess," he adds, "they do with them as the Yankee young ladies do with their live geese—they pluck the feathers off them every spring." All that can be looked for from the pages of this work is an occasional good laugh. The little said of emigration is discouraging.

Charles Joseph Latrobe. "The Rambler in North America." London, 1835. 2 vols. 12mo.

The author ascended the Kennebec from Maine, and by this route reached Quebec. He subsequently visited Three Rivers and Montreal. The volume does not call for any special remark.

Patrick Shireff. "Tour through North America, with a

Comprehensive View of the Canadas and the United States as adapted for Agricultural Emigration." 1835. 8vo.

Mr. Shireff describes himself as a farmer from East Lothian, and his object in visiting the country was to examine its capability of development for agricultural purposes. He visited the Niagara district, York, lake Simcoe, the bay of Quinté, and descended to Montreal. Generally he passed over the whole of the province then accessible to the ordinary traveller. Mr. Shireff expresses his disappointment at what he saw in Canada in comparison with the prosperity he had observed in the United States : an opinion he deliberately repeats at the close of the volume.

Richard Weston. "A Visit to the United States and Canada, 1833; with the view of settling in America. Including a voyage to and from New York." Edinburgh, 1836. pp. 312. 12mo.

Mr. Weston took the precaution on the title page to inform the public that he was a bookseller, " 37 Lothian St., Edinburg." His intention on leaving Scotland was to settle in the United States ; he, however, became depressed by all he saw. He paid a passing visit to Canada, and a few pages record the discontent felt by him. On joining a relative near lake Champlain, he decided to return home. His book is written with the avowed design of cautioning those proposing to emigrate against the exaggerated statements published concerning America.

"A narrative of the affair of Queenston in the war of 1812, with a review of the strictures of that event, in a book entitled ' Notices of the War of 1812.' " New York, 1836. 8vo.

The writer of this volume acted as aide-de-camp to General Stephen Van Rensselaer, in command of the United States forces in 1812 at the battle of Queenston Heights, and he writes in vindicating his chief, in answer to the book of General Ormsbury. The appendix contains many letters which were exchanged between the United States General and Sir Isaac Brock and General Sheaffe. This work commands attention from any writer professing to give a narrative of the action in which the gallant Brock fell, and of the subsequent campaign.

James Inches. "Letters on Emigration to Canada, addressed to the Very Rev. Principal Baird." Second edition. Perth, 1836. 12mo.

This book was avowedly written to discourage emigration, and was published to expose the so-called errors of writers who had favourably described Canada as a field for the industrious effort of all who in the mother country were suffering from adverse circumstances. With this view, it undertook to describe the laborious, profitless life of the emigrant. Emigration, Mr. Inches regarded as an experiment by no means likely to succeed. Wheat raised in Canada, he conceived, would never bring more than the expense of freight and charges. The only place of importance he looked upon with favour was Saint John, New Brunswick.

The problem of changing the scene of life by emigration in order to better one's condition, to turn away from ill fortune to brighter days, *solum vertere*, as Cicero says, seemed beyond his comprehension. Neither could he penetrate the liberty of thought gained in the free air breathed in the forest, untainted by the oft-recurring extravagances of civilization. If there be somewhat rough comfort in the log hut, there is, however, the greatest of human blessings, independence; independence of spirit and a freedom from intercourse with that petty curse of life, the cad, male and female. We have not there to bear

> " the whips and scorns of time,
> The oppressor's wrong, the proud man's contumely,
> The pangs of despised love, the law's delay
> The insolence of office, and the spurns
> That patient merit of the unworthy takes."

No man ever sought communion with nature in vain. Those who live in her contemplation, trusting to their good right arm, never fail to find the sustenance of honesty, and, if true to themselves, obtain their certain reward ; peace of mind, self-respect, health, vigour, and that by which the battle of life is won, endurance. But this philosophy did not suggest itself to Mr. Inches.

Dr. Thomas Rolph, Ancaster Gore District, Dundas, U.C.

"A brief account, together with observations made during a visit in the West Indies, and a tour through the United States of America in parts of the years 1832-3, together with a statistical account of Upper Canada." G. Weyworth Hackslaff, Printer, 1836. 8vo.

The writer sailed from Gravesend, in November, 1832, to Barbadoes, where he continued his journey to the United States. He arrived in Canada, crossing from Black Rock on the 1st June. His work is a general description of the places in Upper Canada he visited, with many incidental statistical letters.

Mrs. Trail. "The backwoods of Canada : being letters from the wife of an emigrant officer." London, 1836.

Mrs. Trail's books are well known. In spite of the hardship and the privation she suffered, she always kept a good heart, looked upon the bright side of life, and conceived a love for Canada she never lost. One sentence is characteristic of her philosophy : "The very stumps that appeared so odious, through long custom seem to lose some of their hideousness ; the eye becomes familiarized even with objects the most displeasing, till they cease to be observed. Some century hence how different will this spot appear !"

Rev. Adolphus Egerton Ryerson, D.D. "The Affairs of the Canadas in a series of Letters to the London *Times*. By a Canadian." London, Eng., 1837. pp. 75.

This work, published anonymously, immediately attracted attention. The consequence was that inquiry at an early period made the name of the author known.

S. S. Hill. "The Emigrant's introduction to an acquaintance with the British American Colonies, and the present condition and prospects of the colonists." London, 1837. 12mo.

The writer commences with the emigration after the flood, and traces the course of colonization through the Phœnicians, the Greeks, and Romans. After a passing glance at Spanish America, he narrates the discoveries of England in the Northern part of the continent, and gives a short history of the former French Canada and the British Provinces. In the second part he describes British America. The advice to emigrants is described as the result of nearly twenty years personal observation. This work, like those of its class, contains several pages of excellent advice, which many an emigrant would have done well to follow.

William Benjamin Wells. "Canadiana: containing sketches of Upper Canada and the Crisis in its Political Affairs. In two parts." London, 1837. pp. 202. 8vo.

Mr. Wells was at the time a journalist and a member of the Upper Canada Legislature. The book carries the impress of his opinions, which were in strong opposition to the government and the policy of Sir Francis Head. Although elected to the house in 1836, Mr. Wells, on the ground of the corrupt practices by which the elections had been carried, refused to take his seat in the session which met on the 8th of November. He proceeded to England to join Robert Baldwin and Duncombe in their protest against the administration of Sir Francis Bond Head. Lord Glenelg refused to receive them ; history must record most unwisely. Mr. Wells therefore ceased to have any political charge. During his stay in England this book was written ; necessarily coloured by his opinions. It is of value as placing on record the political view of the party opposed to the government. It also contains much general information regarding the province, and, as the work is carefully and well written, all who desire to refer to the events of the time can profitably turn to it. There is much strong language at the close of the book, which, no doubt, as years passed on, the author lived to regret. Especially as he rose to a position of some consequence, having been in 1850 appointed judge in the united county of Kent and Lambton, and, on their division, in the county of Kent.

Edward Gibbon Wakefield. " England and America." London, 1837. 2 vols., 8vo.

I have been unable to refer to this work. The first form of this book was published in 1833, in which a comparison was made between the political institutions of Great Britain and the United States. The work of 1837 more fully entered into the question of the relationship of a colony to the parent state. It was probably owing to the opinions Mr. Wakefield expressed in this volume, that he accompanied Lord Durham to Canada in 1838, as private secretary. It is generally admitted that he took a prominent part in the composition of the celebrated Durham report, the production of which exercised so remarkable an influence on Canada. Mr. Wakefield remained in the province after the departure of Lord Durham, as the agent for the Ellice Seigniory, and in the first Legislature of Canada [1841–44] on the retirement of Mr. Dunscombe as member for the County of Beauharnois, in 1842, Mr. Wakefield was elected in his place. Shortly after the termination of this parliament he left Canada. He died in 1862.

Mrs. Jameson. "Winter Studies and Summer Rambles in Canada." 3 vols. London, 1838. Small 8vo.

Mrs. Jameson's book is typified by the words she placed on her title-page, "Leid und Kunst und Scherz," being from the writings of Rahel, the wife of Varnhagen von Ense, the friend of Heine, then much spoken of, who had shortly before died." "Sorrow, Art, and Merriment." We have much of Mrs. Jameson's own experience in connection with literary and artistic thought. We would hardly expect to find in a book on Canada, that the difference between Johnson and Goethe is not greater than that between Eckerman and Boswell. But there are many such parallel passages in connection with a pleasant narrative of her own Canadian experience. Several of Mrs. Jameson's drawings are in the possession of a resident of Toronto, Mr. Robert Bain, having been purchased some years back at the sale of the effects of that lady, viz.: sixty-six pencil sketches contained in a folio scrap book, mostly illustrating views on lakes Erie, Huron and Michigan, with known places in Ontario. They are spoken of as shewing much artistic merit.

Sir George Head. "Forest Scenes and incidents of the wilds of North America, being a diary of a winter's route from Halifax to the Canadas and during four months' residence in the woods on the borders of Lakes Huron and Simcoe." London, 1829. 2nd ed., 1838.

The interest of this book consists in the personal narrative of the writer. The second edition contains a special paper on the question of the north eastern boundary between the territory of Great Britain and the United States, which was then being discussed with some acerbity. It was settled by the Ashburton treaty in August, 1842; one of those diplomatic blunders for which " nobody was to blame." This boundary, so prejudicial to Canada, arose from the error of the British Commissioners in 1797, accepting the tributary stream Chiputnaticook, the eastern branch of the main river, when the western branch, called the Schoodic, should have been followed. Had the latter been so accepted, the boundary would have been carried one hundred miles south of its present location, by which 11,000 square miles would have been gained by the dominion ; a line undoubtedly in accordance with the Treaty of 1783.

Rt. Hon. Sir William Molesworth. " Speech on the Canada Bill, 23rd January, 1838." London, 1838. 8vo.

Sir William Molesworth in 1853 was appointed first commissioner of public works, and, 1855, became secretary for the colonies. He died in October of that year at the early age of 45.

James Logan, advocate. "Notes of a Journey through Canada, the United States of America and the West Indies." Edinburgh, 1838. 12mo.

Mr. Logan landed at Quebec in July, 1836, ascended the Saint Lawrence to Montreal, and finally made his way to Goderich, from which place he descended Lake Huron to Detroit. The book is a record of what was then experienced on this journey of a few days, for Mr. Logan reached Detroit in September.

" Six years in the Bush ; or extracts from the journal of a settler in Upper Canada, 1832–1838." London, 1838. Small 8vo.

The writer of this book, a university man, on leaving Oxford, resolved to try his fortune in America. His opinions may be judged by the words of Coleridge, which he placed on the title page. They are not generally known, so they are repeated here :—" Colonization is not only a manifest expedient, but an imperative duty on Great Britain. God seems to hold his finger out to us over the sea. But it must be a national colonization, such as was that of the Scotch to America : a colonization of *Hope*, and not such as we alone have encouraged and effected for the last fifty years, a colonization of *Despair.*" Furnished with letters and possessing means, he found little romance in his new career. He went to the Talbot settlement and to Lake Simcoe ; but circumstances determined his choice of the township of Verulam, where he purchased 3,000 acres, not far from Fenelon Falls. Peterboro was for a time his headquarters. From this spot he went to a ball in Cobourg ; in those days no common matter, in the elastic period of youth, for a sleigh load of beauty with its attendant cavaliers to drive some twenty or thirty miles to be present on such an occasion ; he went likewise to a "bachelors' ball" at Peterboro, which, by the brief allusion to it, appears to have been a great success. He records with more detail the opening of a church in the settlement. He describes how they commenced with the "Morning hymn." It is surprising, in my humble judgment, how this old English hymn of the conscientious non-juror bishop Ken, has passed out of use in the Church of England, to be supplanted by much of the dubious sentimentality of modern hymnology. Perhaps some Broad-church clergyman may see the wisdom of restoring it to use. The volume may be described as a pleasant record of personal adventure, and in the sense of bringing back to us "the sixty years since," it is useful for reference in any description of the time.

L. de Wette. "Reise in den Vereingten Staaten und Canada im Jahr, 1837." Leipzig, 1838. 8vo.

William Bettridge, B.D. "A brief history of the church in Upper Canada ; containing the acts of parliament, imperial and provincial ; royal instructions ; proceedings of the deputation ; correspondence with the government ; Clergy Reserves question, &c., &c." London, 1838. 8vo.

Mr. Bettridge, of St. John's College, Cambridge, was the Rector of Woodstock, Upper Canada, and in this work writes as a defender of the "Clergy Reserves" in the interest of his church. He was one of the deputation that in 1837 proceeded to England, to make known "to the authorities of Church and State, as also to the

Clergy and Laity generally, the state of absolute privation of the ministrations of our holy religion." Mr. Bettridge relates the result of his mission, and in his narrative publishes many documents, in which the "Clergy Reserves" question is discussed from his point of view.

E. Rosier. "The Emigrant's friend in Canada." London, 1839. 18mo.

I have not been able to find this book.

Sir Francis Bond Head, Bart. "A Narrative." London, 1839. 488pp. App. A, 13. B. Stanton, Toronto, 38.

It falls to my duty to notice this particular work of this brilliant *litterateur*, for it is a narrative of his government of Upper Canada from January, 1836, to March, 1838. There was probably no similar political event as his appointment to the position. He himself has graphically related all the strange circumstances connected with it ; and he adds somewhat naïvely, "I was really grossly ignorant of everything that in any way related to the government of the colonies" (p. 25). Sir Francis Hincks in his " Reminiscences of his public life " (p. 14) on the authority of Mr. Roebuck asserts that the letter of appointment was addressed by lord Glenelg, then colonial secretary, to the wrong person. It had been determined to discontinue the nomination of military governors, and lord Lansdowne had recommended Sir Edmund Head ; by error the letter was addressed to Sir Francis Bond Head. Sir Francis Hincks adds that he was confirmed in this opinion by "the positive assurance of the correctness of the statement by a distinguished imperial statesman." In private conversation Sir Francis expressed his conviction of its entire truth.

It is not my purpose in this place to enter into the consideration of Head's administration. It is far too complex a question to be considered in a few sentences. This, however, may be said, whatever the error of his public career, no one has assailed his desire to do right, or the worth of his personal character. He was selected to hold the balance between two extreme political parties, each marked by extreme arrogance and unyielding opinions, neither understanding, even in a minor degree, the tolerance so indis-

G

pensable to political life, and alike unbending in the advocacy of the policy each advocated. Moreover, to add to the complications, there was a weak, incompetent, colonial minister, whose theory of government was to get rid of, rather than to meet an embarrassing question. It was likewise a period of transition, and Head, although possessing ability and force of character, was without true political sagacity, and he had not passed through the training, by which this want is to some extent supplied. All his opinions were entertained with passionate earnestness, and they were entirely at variance with the requirements of Canada. His remedy was to stem all democratic spirit as he put it (p. 281) in his despatch of the 10th Sept., 1837, to "oppose its progress."

Head refused to carry out the instructions of the colonial office, viz., to place Mr. Bidwell on the bench, and to restore Mr. George Ridout to a judgeship. He gave his reasons in a despatch of unusual length, (10th Sept.) and in doing so tendered his resignation. It was not accepted until the 26th of January, 1838, when Sir George Arthur was appointed to succeed him. Head left Canada the following March.

This work, "a narrative," we are told, was printed in one week. It appeared a year after his return to England. His primary view was the vindication of his character and government; in this he attained a certain success, for it is not possible to read the book without extending to its writer a certain sympathy; he certainly lost no consideration by its appearance. There is no work better known to the historical student: one reason is that it is readable, and even in his abuse of his opponents Head is straightforward and fearlessly expresses his opinions. He doubtless looked upon his government of Canada with a feeling he could himself scarcely describe; for if on one side he awoke extreme discontent, in the opposite direction he called forth much devotion. Head must be always looked upon as one of the many men sent to carry out a trying duty, when success is only possible with statesmen of high, noble and chivalrous qualities, in connection with unfailing, unsleeping judgment. It is only an act of justice to criticize his government with the consideration of its great complications. Whatever his faults, he was devoted to the British Empire, and had a keen sentiment regarding its glory and greatness. His feeling with regard to his own career may, perhaps, be truly expressed by the

lines he placed on the title page, those of Æneas when he commenced his narrative to Dido of the ruin and destruction of Troy.
Quamquam animus meminisse horret luctuque refugit ;
Incipiam.

T. R. Preston. "Three years' residence in Canada, from 1837, to 1839 ; with a review of the condition of the Canadian people, &c., &c." London, 1840. 2 vols., 8vo.

This book appeared after the two rebellions of 1837, 1838, when things had somewhat quieted. An account is given of the events of those days, not, however, in a connected form ; and many of the prominent topics of the day are considered. This work may be principally referred to, as shewing the sentiment of the class of persons which the writer represented.

Charles Buller. "Responsible Government for Colonies." London, 1840.

Mr. Buller was one of the many able men who accompanied lord Durham to Canada. He sat in the house of Commons from 1832 until his death in 1848. He obtained a high reputation as a contributor to the reviews of his day.

I cannot pretend that the list I have given of the books bearing upon Canada within the sixty years from 1783 to 1840 published outside the province is complete, even within the limit I have observed. I may claim, however, that it has been my effort to make it as comprehensive as possible. Among the works excluded are the pamphlets, which on occasions have been numerous. Many have entirely disappeared and remain unknown even by name ; in some instances, no copy being extant, the work is unremembered. It is possible that no perfect list can be given of these *brochures* without reference to the collection in the British Museum, and it would prove a work of no ordinary labour and

Note Æ. II. 12. Although my mind shudders to remember [the past] and takes refuge in grief ; I will begin.

research. It is difficult to draw a precise and defined line where the classification of the pamphlet should cease, and the higher class of work commence : often the so-called volumes are merely expanded pamphlets, while, on the other hand, a few well digested, carefully written pages may deservedly claim a reputation, to which many a bulky volume cannot aspire.

I cannot accuse myself of want of endeavour to make the calendar full and reliable, so far as the sources available for reference permitted me. Some of my literary friends, I fear, may unpleasantly remember the pertinacity with which I troubled them by inquiries. My sources of information have been the Parliamentary Library, the Archive branch at Ottawa and the city of Toronto Library. I must express my thankfulness to the gentlemen connected with these institutions, Mr. Sylvain, Dr. Brymner, and Mr. James Bain, for the assistance I have received from them, and for the forbearance with which they entertained my appeals to their attention. I must specially acknowledge the kindness and consideration shewn me by Mr. Bain, and the great assistance he rendered me.

In cases where no account is given of the calendared volume, I have been unable to gain access to it.

I have alluded to the Archives in a previous portion of this work. I conceive that I may with propriety give some account of the Parliamentary Library in Ottawa, and of the leading libraries in Ontario.

The original library of the Province of Canada in 1841

was formed from the two libraries of the provinces of Upper and Lower Canada. There was no very particular effort to increase its capacity in the early years of the United Province, and the additions to it were but moderate. During the Montreal riots arising from the Rebellion Losses act, on the 25th of April, 1849, the Parliament House was senselessly burnt by the mob, composed to a great extent of idlers and boys, as such a rabble is generally constituted. No evidence could be obtained how this outrage was committed. Whatever the excitement of public feeling, the act at the time was regarded as unpremeditated; and it remains one of the many proofs that, when a crowd begins to set law at defiance, and is unchecked in the first ebullition of mischievous folly, it is hard to tell to what excess it will not proceed. The madness of the proceeding is in itself a proof that, if an intentional act, it was the work of some of those reckless hangers-on of tumult in any form, who appear upon any public commotion. There was, however, at the time a current belief that it arose from some escape of gas. The fire raged with such rapidity that it was scarcely possible to remove anything from the building. One significant act took place, the successful effort to save the Queen's portrait, which had been lately painted by Partridge, and there was a general concurrence in effecting its preservation. It now hangs in the House of Commons at Ottawa; but the romance connected with its presence seems to have been generally forgotten. Perhaps these few words may aid in revivifying the remembrance of it. The library, however, with the exception of some odd volumes, was entirely destroyed.

The material loss to the province was sufficiently serious, viewed in its estimate of money. The furniture of the building; an almost entire library of books; the printed

# 102

records; with much of the private property of the members of the House and the officers of the Legislature. The loss, however serious, was resolvable into figures; but there was much destroyed that indeed was irreparable. Early examples of printing in the first years of the province of Upper Canada had been inherited from the library of that province, in some instances to be found nowhere else; they forever disappeared. The Lower Canada section was rich in many MSS. and records of French rule, which in past years had been gathered by Mr. Faribault. This fine collection was burned; in the half-century which has elapsed, for the period is close upon that time, in spite of constant attention and effort to make the loss in all respects good, it is feared that much must remain unreplaced, several of the books and MSS. not being procurable.*

The consequence of these riots was the removal of the seat of government from Montreal where they took place, and the establishment of the absurd system of the perambulating change of location; four years being passed in Toronto, and four in Quebec. The succeeding legislature accordingly met in Toronto in May, 1850, and continued there during 1851, when the change was made to Quebec. This system lasted fifteen years, alternating between the two cities. It was found to be cumbersome in every respect, leading to great expense, and failing in its object to extend advantage to the cities, which could agree on no other policy

---

* Mr. Faribault has left on record his wide reading and knowledge in this respect, in the work published by him at Quebec in 1837: "Catalogue d'ouvrages sur l'histoire de l'Amérique, et en particulier sur celle du Canada, de la Louisiane, de l'Acadie, et d'autres lieux, ci-devant connus sous le nom de la Nouvelle-France. Avec des notes bibliographiques, critiques et littéraires." The volume is now somewhat rare.

regarding the seat of government, but its constant change. Finally, after much political difficulty, which in no way I feel called upon to narrate, Ottawa was named as the seat of government, and on the 8th of June, 1866, the legislature met in the new parliamentary buildings.*

But the misfortunes of the perambulating government were not finished, and in their train the library was again a sufferer. On the 1st of February, 1854, the House of Assembly at Quebec was destroyed by fire. Commissioners were appointed to inquire into the cause, and, as indeed might have been expected, no evidence was forthcoming to warrant a positive opinion on the subject. The testimony of the witnesses was reported at length, and the public was left to

---

* The following are the dates of the change :—

| | | | | |
|---|---|---|---|---|
| 1850 | Toronto. | House assembled, | | 14th May. |
| 1851 | | | | |

| | | | | |
|---|---|---|---|---|
| 1852 | Quebec. | " | " | 19th August. |
| 3 | | | | |
| 4 | | | | |
| 5 | | | | |

| | | | | |
|---|---|---|---|---|
| 1856 | Toronto. | " | " | 15th February. |
| 7 | | | | |
| 8 | | | | |
| 9 | | | | |

| | | | | |
|---|---|---|---|---|
| 1860 | Quebec. | " | " | 28th February. |
| 1 | | | | |
| 2 | | | | |
| 3 | | | | |
| 4 | | | | |
| 5 | | " | " | 19th January. |

The last session held at Quebec.

1866

8th June.   The first session at Ottawa.

form its own conclusions. There is, however, ground for
belief that the fire was attributable to defective flues. It
was first discovered in the early morning about three o'clock
on the 1st of February, in a new wing lately constructed,
and before assistance could be obtained it made rapid
progress. Many alterations in the building had been hastily
carried out, and little precaution had been taken against the
possibility of fire. The messengers had examined the rooms
before leaving the building, and there was no discovery of
any want of care. The mode of heating the building was
pronounced to have been in no way the cause of the fire,
direct or indirect, and the commissioners added their
unhesitating opinion that the burning was purely the result
of accident and not of design.*

We learn from the commissioners' report some facts connected with the library  At the last examination the library
consisted of 17,000 volumes, which had been collected at an
expense of £10,000 ($40,000). A great number of books
had been received as donations, and, including such volumes,
the actual value of the library was established at £11,723
($46,892). Of the 17,000 volumes on the shelves at the
period of the fire, 8,725 were preserved. As the library was
insured for $40,000, no loss resulted to the province in this
respect, there being an amount sufficient to replace the
missing books. The loss on the building and furniture,
deducting the insurance, was $150,000.

It is a curious fact to commemorate that the catastrophe
was repeated some weeks subsequently. The House of

* "Report of the commissioners appointed to inquire into the
cause of the fire at the parliament buildings on the 1st of February,
1854, and the circumstances connected therewith. J. W. Dunscomb
and Oliver Fiset, Esquires, commissioners ; Geo. Futvoye, Esquire,
secretary, Quebec, 1854." The report is dated 27th February.

Assembly had been so thoroughly destroyed that the government hired the convent of the Sisters of Charity near the glacis by Saint John's gate, fronting on St. Olivier street. On the night of the 3rd of May this edifice was discovered to be on fire, which continued until the building was gutted and unfit for occupation. Workmen were engaged upon the premises at the time, and, as but little of the government furniture had been moved there, in this respect there was scarcely any loss. As the books had not been transferred the library was in no way a sufferer. The consequence of this second fire was that the Music Hall in Saint Louis street was hired for the use of the legislative assembly, and the Court House was assigned to the council.* The library was installed in the building in Saint Louis street, opposite the Music Hall.

Parliament met on the 13th of June. This narrative not being a political treatise, it is only necessary to remark that Mr. Cauchon moved an amendment to the address, expressing regret that the seigneurial question had not been considered, to which Mr. Sicotte supplemented an expression of regret, that the clergy reserves had been left unmentioned in view of their secularization. The amendment was carried by a vote of 42 to 24. It was a vote of want of confidence. The majority comprehended the most opposite elements, and Lord Elgin, on the advice of his ministry, on the 20th of the

---

* A commission consisting of Mr. R. S. M. Bouchette and Mr. Dunbar Ross was appointed to examine into the causes of the accident. They reported on the 19th of June, but were unable to come to any conclusion. At the date of the fire 150 carpenters and joiners were actively employed in the building. Their duty being limited to this inquiry, no other point is touched upon. [Vol. 13, 1st Sess. V. parliament, 1854-5, No. 7.] The *Quebec Chronicle* of the 6th states : "The Legislature had removed very few of its effects to the building, and had therefore lost little."

month took the political world by surprise by proroguing the
House. A general election followed. Parliament met on
the 5th of September and sat until the 18th of December,
when it adjourned until the 23rd of February, 1855. The
sittings were continued until the 30th of May. The next
session was held at Toronto on the 15th of February, 1856.

The journals of Parliament record the thanks of the House
to the archbishop, the ecclesiastics of the seminary, and the
military for their exertions in saving a portion of the library.
Thanks were voted to the emperor of the French for the
munificent donation made by the French government; to the
houses of lords and commons, the lord chancellor and
speaker of the house of commons, and to several societies
and private gentlemen for their contributions. Also, to the
president of the United States and the governors and legislatures of New York, Connecticut, Pennsylvania, Ohio,
Maine, Vermont, Virginia, Michigan, Louisiana, Massachusetts
and New Hampshire, and to others. The librarian was also
sent to England to make purchases to replace the books
destroyed.

It cannot be said that much was done to bring the library
to a high state of efficiency during the remaining years that
the " perambulation " took place. The Government remained
in Toronto until 1859. In 1860 the legislature was again at
Quebec. There was no further move to Toronto. Ottawa
had been finally established as the seat of government, and
the legislature remained at Quebec until permanently transferred to the new capital. The last session held at Quebec
opened on the 19th of January, 1865, and closed the 30th of
June. On the 8th of June, 1866, the first parliament was
opened at Ottawa. It was the last parliament of the old
province of Canada.

It is from the period of confederation that the library

may be said to date the commencement of its present
excellence. As the books increased, it was soon seen that the
provision made for the library was totally inadequate ; consequently the present circular structure, originally designed by
Mr. Thomas Fuller, was placed under contract : the interior
arrangement being that of Mr. Thomas S. Scott, chief archi-
tect, public works. Being completed, without fixtures, in
1876, shortly after the still well remembered fancy ball of
lord Dufferin, a ball was given there, if my memory does not
fail me, by Mr. Cauchon, then speaker of the Senate. In
a short time afterwards the library fittings were completed
and the books transferred to them. No one can stand in
this noble hall without being impressed with the dignity of its
appearance, and its extent. The liberality of the legislature,
however, and the desire on every side to make the parliamentary library worthy the country, have led to a most liberal
expenditure, and already the pressure of insufficient room is
felt. It is very certain, if the library is to retain its character,
that additional room must be found. I will not take upon
myself to say in what form. It is a subject which demands
much consideration. When these additions are made, they
should be of sufficient extent to last for a century. Those
who have carefully studied the question have no doubt
definite views of what is required, and the subject has to be
approached in an enlarged spirit, narrowed by no false
economy, or unwise limitation. If I hesitate to express
an opinion as to the course to be followed, it is not from
any want of faith in the necessity of the enlargement. It
is a fact patent to every man of letters admitted to the
library, and those senators and members of parliament
who have considered the question are fully impressed with
the sense of the obligation which in this respect lies upon
the government.

The present unsatisfactory condition of the library arises from its very wealth. It possesses so many volumes as to be cramped for room: the shelves are crowded, and the search for a book is often embarrassing. There is a class of people who may say, then buy no more books. That is one remedy, it is true; but it can be carried out only at the cost of lagging behind all modern thought; by remaining ignorant of the discoveries of science; by failing to go onward with the advance of art; by ceasing to occupy the front rank in the elevating pursuit of literature. If we do not tremble at the appearance of a comet,[*] if we know the benefit of drainage to avoid disease, if we have no plagues of the middle ages, if we no longer believe in the charlatanism which finds coal at Quebec and Bowmanville, if we learn that there is something higher in life than making money, and being a trickster and a perjurer in politics, if we have law based on sense and reason, it is because we have books, to teach us what is right, materially and morally. We may count, therefore, on the general assent that the library must be continued at its present high standard of excellence. If this theory is to be maintained, greater library accommodation must be obtained. It is a matter not without difficulty, but it is by no means insuperable. It is not one lightly or flippantly to be approached, for it demands much reflection, and prudence and judgment have to be exercised in determining the course to be followed. One fact may be relied upon, that the proposition would command such universal countenance, that those inclined to oppose the augmentation would generally hesitate to assert themselves, if animated by a love of popularity.

I will, however, take upon myself to suggest an arrange-

[*] It is only two centuries back that Boyle wrote his "Pensées diverses écrites à un Docteur de Sorbonne à l'occasion de la comète qui parut au mois de Décembre, 1680."

ment, which would for some years greatly relieve the present pressure, and which is desirable in many points of view, especially from the accommodation it would extend to the more studious senators and members of parliament; those who refer to law authorities, and fit themselves for debate. It is to convert the present reading room into a law library, and, keeping it *au courant* of all literature of this class, place it in charge of an able, educated sub-librarian, who would take charge of the branch, with a sufficient number of assistants to attend to the mechanical labour of fetching books. The remedy is as inexpensive as it would prove efficient. Where, it may be said, would you establish the reading room? It is not my duty to examine into that point, and, were it so, I would hesitate to express an opinion, without a full consideration of every interest involved. I am told, on what I regard as good authority, that there would be no difficulty in that direction. The situation of the present reading room, it must be recollected, was that of the first library, and, as we regard it at this date, one cannot but feel how ridiculously small it was for the original purpose intended. From this fact, however, it is directly accessible both from the senate and house of commons, and in that point of view presents admirable advantages for the use suggested. The establishment of such an *addendum* should be regulated according to the strictest rules. It should be regarded as if it were a close literary club: no one admitted, except a senator or a member of the lower house, without a joint written order from the speakers, and then only under exceptional circumstances. Out of the session the admission could be more general, under certain rules. This arrangement would for a time, independently of the benefit it would extend to the higher class of members, greatly relieve the pressure in the library. It would exact no large disbursement to effect the change, and

I think it may be safely said, it would in no way lead to inconvenience.

Possibly these recommendations may arouse so much attention, that the change will be enforced by public opinion, although it is without promise of political support to the ministry.

I have now to turn to the condition and extent of the library itself, in which every branch of science, art, literature and law is to be found; the collection numbers 150,000 distinct works, entered upon the catalogue. The number of volumes which they represent is difficult to determine. Those who are learned in averages may draw their own conclusions on this point. They have been estimated roughly at a quarter of a million.

A large portion of the annual appropriation so liberally voted by parliament is devoted to the acquisition of works upon law, social and political economy, political history, history and statistics, and *belles lettres.* The political section likewise receives a great increase from the exchanges received from foreign governments; a recognized system, both courteous and useful, by which all libraries are greatly benefited. Thus, the collection in this respect is not only enriched by the parliamentary papers and reports of Great Britain, France and the United States, but also from many of the states of the Union, and the greater number of the British colonies.

The historical student will find no want unsatisfied in his research. A rare collection of books, French and English, necessary to investigation, is available for use; it includes as far as possible, all that recent research has brought to light; the publications issued under the authority of the Master of the Rolls in the mother country: " La collection des Documents Inédits," published by the French government; the works brought out by "La Société de l'histoire de France;" "American Archives," edited by Peter Force; also, the publications of the societies devoted to the exploration of Palestine and Egypt, which have in the last few years thrown great light on several of the knotty points of ancient history, with the splendid fac-similes of papyri issued by the British Museum of the works of Schliemann, de Cesnola and others.

Especial care is taken in the collections bearing upon the history of the northern continent of America. I would be ungrateful if I failed to bear testimony to its excellence and to the courtesy extended to me in reference to it. In the two fires which I have recorded, the greatest loss experienced in the library was the destruction of documents of this class, the void of which is still felt in spite of every effort made to replace them. Generally the works I have calendared were from the shelves of the library. In the instances when I failed to meet with them, Dr. Brymner and Mr. Bain, of the Toronto library, came to my rescue with characteristic courtesy and kindness.

The inventor and patent-seeker can complain of no lack of sources of information in the richness of the collection which lies at their disposal. They will find a complete set of the specifications of the patents granted in the United Kingdom, France, the United States, with those of the leading British provinces in the outer empire. The above are supplemented by the official and non-official reports of the International, Intercolonial, and the other leading exhibitions held since 1850.

The series of the proceedings and transactions of the learned societies of the United Kingdom, France, and the United States are to be found generally complete, likewise the leading reviews, magazines, and the chief periodicals of those countries.

The section of the fine arts may be asserted to be, without undue praise or exaggeration, unsurpassed on the continent. For the past years it has been developed with much good taste and judgment. Among its most valuable examples may be mentioned the "Chalcographie du Musée du Louvre," from the library of Louis Philippe, king of the French, in 81 volumes; "Gavard's Galeries historiques," with supplement, 17 volumes; the "Musée Français;" the "Annales du Musée et de l'École moderne des Beaux Arts;" the publications of the "Arundel Society;" autotype production of the works of Raphael and the great painters of modern times; "Stodart's drawings of the Bayeux Tapestry;" Wagner's "Treasures of Art in Great Britain;" John Ruskin's works; Hogarth; masterpieces of French, German and Italian art; Holbein's "Dance of Death;" the Chatsworth Raffaelles; reproductions of Landseer, Millais, Whistler, and of most of the known modern artists.

The Greek and Latin classics, although not rich in ancient and renowned editions, make a good exhibit. The last imprints of modern scholarship are well represented, all the new editions being obtained, as they appear, to be added to the list: such works as those of Jowett, Jebb, Conington and men of their class. There is to be found "Valpy's Classics," edition of 1830; "Bohn's classical library;" "La collection des Auteurs Grecs," with the Latin translation, published by the great firm of Firmin, Didot of Paris; the collection published by Panckoucke, with French translation, and several minor editions.

In German and Italian the principal standard authors only are to be found. They consist chiefly of the classical poets and *belles-lettres*. The readers in this branch of literature have been so exceedingly limited as in no way to suggest great expenditure in this direction. In German, however,

113

the works bearing in any way on the American revolutionary war are present for reference.* The best known English translations of the standard authors of Germany and Italy represent this branch of literature.

During the past years no effort has been spared to procure the earliest and best editions of all English standard works, both in prose and poetry. It is not always an easy matter to reach this result; catalogues have to be studied, and much attention and correspondence are necessary to attain success. These books are only to be obtained as opportunity offers, and not unfrequently the order arrives too late for the purchase. Full success in this design must be a matter of time and constant watchfulness.

The editions of Shakespeare with the commentaries on his plays constitute a small library in themselves. It is painful to add that many of these sets are imperfect. It may be said that it is in this direction the greatest ravages in past years have been made by those who have the *right* to take books from the library. Several of the editions have been disgracefully mutilated, and are incomplete. It is not only in this direction that this remark applies. The classical library has greatly suffered. Books have disappeared from the shelves, many of which were authoritatively obtained, and remain unreturned. Sir John Abbott, if he has not abandoned the studies of his youth, in which he obtained some distinction, may possibly feel himself called upon, when these deficiencies in the classics are brought to

<hr>

* The latest addition is " Schlösser's Letters," in 28 volumes. A portion of their contents have lately been translated by Mr. W. L. Stone, of New Jersey. "Brief Wechsel meist historischen und politischen Inhalts. August Ludwig Schlösser [1776-1782]. Gottingen, 10 vols. Staats Anzeigen Gesammelt von August Ludwig Schlösser. Vol. I., 1772. Vol. XVIII., 1793. 18 vols.

his attention, to see that steps are taken to supply the loss. He is the one member of the present ministry who can be appealed to, for no other has any knowledge of these studies, or the least sympathy with them. There are some members of the senate and house of commons who may feel interested in this appeal, and who may consider it a duty to intervene in this emergency. The fact that many valuable works have been rendered imperfect must be stated without circumlocution, and also that books of the library have been discreditably injured and mutilated.

There ought to be a stringent law, that valuable books of a high order should on no account be permitted to leave the walls of the library, even at the demand of the highest personage in the Dominion. They should only be open to reference within the building. It is at variance with sense and propriety, that these volumes should be placed in the hands of any persons who are ignorant of their value, and who are indifferent as to the treatment which they receive. It is a point, concerning which no privilege should be pleaded, for it is, on occasions, exercised only in mischief. I court an inquiry into the matter, so that it may be seen if in any respect I misrepresent or exaggerate.

The admirable manner in which the catalogue is kept is deserving of special allusion. In the first place, the caligraphy is such that the absence of printer's type is never missed; not always a feature in catalogues. It consists of two divisions of books : one in which the works are entered in their classification, as they are received; the other, in which authors are recorded alphabetically, with reference made to the full title of their work, and the shelf where each volume is to be found. A reader may thus learn in the simplest manner, by turning to the register, if the name of the author sought for is on the catalogue; and the place where the work is accessible.

There has been some attempt of late years to "simplify" cataloguing, as it is called, so as to reduce the labour of entry; one of which is to insert the name of the author on a card, and place it in a drawer in its alphabetical position. This system has found great favour in many libraries of the United States, and has been to a great extent brought into use. By many it is claimed as a modern improvement, capable of the fullest expansion, as being easy of reference and getting rid of much, as its advocates qualify it, useless labour. Saving the last adjective, it may be admitted that this result is in a way obtained, and, from the view of the official in the library, may be perhaps sustained by additional argument. But is not this beside the question? A librarian is not at the head of his staff as an ornamental personage. To my mind, his first function is a higher one than simply discovering the easiest mode in which he can perform his duty. His obligation is undoubtedly to govern the library wisely, and discreetly expend the money confided to him; but the library itself has been established and is endowed for the benefit of the student, for the readers who refer to its volumes. The primary question, then, to my mind, is not what gives the least trouble to the officials, but what is the most effective way of giving information to those seeking it. Like everything else in life, there is no royal road to a perfect catalogue, and the one consideration is, not the amount of labour, or the simplicity of the system on which it may be made, but the means by which information can be readily obtained by those looking for it. The written alphabetical catalogue, kept up to the latest edition, can be referred to by anyone who can read and write. On this subject it may be said there are two classes of persons who have recourse to these volumes : the one that patiently and reverently turns over the leaves, careful to avoid injury ;

and the very opposite, those negligent, reckless examiners, who, considering only their own momentary want, carelessly and hastily persevere in their search, indifferent as to the injury they inflict on the pages they are consulting. Such semi-barbarians, at least in this point of view, should be debarred the use of the library. By this mode of examination, *i.e.*, reference to the catalogue, the information desired on any subject is gained in the easiest and most rapid manner. The card system is tedious, cumbersome and fatiguing for reference by the student. In every well-conducted library the works are classified : the consequence is, that with the best intention a mistake may be made and a book unwisely catalogued, and so escape attention, being placed in the wrong class. In an alphabetical index, where name succeeds name regardless of the subject, and reference is made to the volume of classification, where the title of the book is given in full, such a mischance is impossible.

I am quite aware that the opinions I express will be controverted by many men of ability and reputation. I am not, however, unacquainted with libraries, and my remarks may claim some attention, from the experience which has suggested them. The system of cataloguing in the parliamentary library, in my humble judgment, is most satisfactory, and in every respect reflects the highest credit on the gentlemen in charge of it.

Some mention must be made of the Canadian coinage in the library. It is not kept in cabinets, but placed under glass cases, so that it may be remarked by the many holiday visitors who enter the library. It is well arranged in this form as one of the sights by the custodian, Mr. Casault. Care is taken by him to keep it up to the latest standard. There are many medals annually struck to record passing events, especially in connection with the Roman catholic societies, and to perpetuate the merits of some enterprising trader. Every numismatist remembers the copper tokens of the mother country. Those of the time of Charles I., issued between 1640 and 1660, have been catalogued by Mr. Boyle. Ten thousand specimens are recorded ; it is believed that the total issue exceeded double this number. The remarkable Beaufoy collection, belonging to the corporation of imperial London, is set forth in a work of unusual learning and ability. What are called the Conder tokens, from the name of the person who has catalogued them, were issued towards the close of the last century. They first appeared in 1798 and died out in 1801. Without varieties and "mules," there are about 1,200 tokens which can be legitimately so considered. Conder catalogues 2,400. The later copper tokens, which appeared between 1810-15, remain uncatalogued ; the silver tokens of the date have been placed on record. This branch of numismatics is a study in itself.

Those who have never looked into the matter will be surprised to learn that Canada has a literature in this respect. The first book printed on the subject was by Mr. Alfred Sandham, " Coins, Tokens and Medals of the Dominion," Montreal, 1869.

Mr. Sandham was in this respect the instrument of reducing our numismatic chaos to order. Many writers have followed him, the last being Dr. Leroux, whose volume appears to be the standard book. Collectors, however, say that it is not "das buch der Zukunft;" 1854 pieces are catalogued. They include what is known of the coinage during the French *régime*, current in New France. The special coinage for Canada, however, was not important at this date.*

---

* The latest authority on the pieces issued, previous to the

In the form in which the medals and coins are kept, they are well arranged, and much attention has been bestowed to keep the collection *au courant* of the latest pieces struck in the Dominion, and in obtaining examples of the coinage current during French rule. The collection bids fair to be as

conquest, by France for Canada and the colonies, is E. Zay, "Histoire Monétaire des Colonies Françaises d'après les documents Officiels, avec 278 figures." Paris, 1892. I am indebted to Mr. Casault for reference to this volume. They are as follows :—

### FOR THE COLONIES GENERALLY.

(1.) Piece de 15 sols (silver).
    LUD. XIIII., D.G. (soleil), FR. ET. NAV. REX.
    R. GLORIAM REGNI TUI DICENT, 1670. Ex. A.

(2.) The same piece, smaller. 5 sols.

(3.) A pattern piece at Paris, never issued. Copper.
    LUDOVICUS XIIII., D. G. R., FRAN. ET. NAV. REX.
    In field 16 L. 70, under a crown A.
    R. in four lines, DOUBLE | DE LA | MERIQUE | FRAN-
    CAISE. Ex. A. 3. *Fleurs-de-lis.*

(4.) Copper.
    LUD. XV., D. G., FR. ET NAV. REX.
    R. XII. DENIERS COLONIES, 1717. Ex. Q.

(5.) The same mint for
    VI. DENIERS.

(6.) Copper.
    SIT NOMEN DOMINI BENEDICTUM.
    2 L. [*en sautoir, couronnés.*]
    R. COLONIES FRANCAISES, 1721. Ex. H.

(7.) Billon.
    In field C. crowned, the legend not decipherable, marked
    on one side only.

(8.) Double sol de 24 deniers.
    L. crowned with 3 *fleurs-de-lis* in field.
    LUD. XV., D. G., FR. ET. NAV. REX. Ex. A fox.
    R. SIT NOM. DOM. BENEDICTUM. 1738. Ex. A.
    2 L. *affrontées et croisées.* Crown above.

perfect as it can be made. At present it is weak on one or two sections, especially with regard to the sacramental tokens. It is to be hoped that no opportunity which offers for legitimately completing this national collection will be allowed to pass by. It is, likewise, worthy of consideration whether it be not advisable to place the medals and coins in the orthodox cabinet, instead of leaving them under glass cases, as is the practice in the modern ten-cent museum.* According to Mr. Casault the Canadian coins number 731, the medals, 546; making a total of 1,277.

I have spoken of the sacramental tokens. Mr. R. W. McLachlan, of Montreal, last year published a thin volume, but of much use to the Canadian numismatist, "Canadian Communion Tokens," a catalogue of metal sacramental tickets used in the different Presbyterian churches in Canada. Mr. McLachlan is the pioneer in this branch of the science; he gives a catalogue of 241 such tokens. The labour of gaining the information must have been a serious matter, for it was only derivable by direct correspondence with the ministers of the several churches. These tokens, in the first instance, arose with the Scotch Presbyterians, and were subsequently accepted by the reformed churches of France. They were never used in England and Ireland. No doubt the custom took its origin in Scotland from its necessity. The population at the time was scattered; the sacrament was only administered at long intervals on a given date, and many

---

* Independently of the charge of the coins, Mr. Casault is responsible for the care of the library with the books, and has many varied duties to perform; among them is that of dispensing the stationery. The latter, however, in modern times, is not a weighty office; for out of the session even one sheet of paper cannot be obtained by a reader in the library, without special humble application.

communicants travelled long distances in order to be present. The production of the ticket was a proof of worthiness to be admitted to the rite. These tickets are of many descriptions of form and size, and are made of copper, brass, white metal, and even of silver.

According to Mr. McLachlan, the earliest known Canadian token is that of Truro, Nova Scotia, formerly Cobequid. It was at this spot the first organized Presbyterian church was established in British America. The earliest Montreal token is dated 1803. It is from the church organized by the Rev. John Bethune in 1788, which met in the old Recollet church in Notre Dame street until 1792, when the first St. Gabriel church was built. The oldest known token of Canada is that of 1794, in use by the Glengarry settlers.*

It is a most agreeable duty to record the re-establishment of the library of Toronto University, in a period so short as to call for wonderment at its re-creation. It may be remembered that only sixteen months have elapsed since the destruction of the whole building by fire, on the 14th of February, 1890, when the interior of the main building, including the convocation hall and library, was completely gutted, the walls alone remaining standing. The library, admirably selected, then contained about 33,000 volumes, including many valuable editions of the Greek and Latin classics, which the scholarship and the good taste of the first president, Dr. McCaul, had led him to collect. The interior of the library was particularly striking, all the

---

*The Scottish tokens have been catalogued by the Rev. Thomas Burns, P.S.A., Edinburgh. The United States tokens by Mr. Thomas Warner, New York.

compartments having been built of carved oak, the whole of excellent architectural effect. The extraordinary energy shewn in the restoration of the building, the walls having remained generally without injury, permitted the recommencement of university work last October, the students according to their university years returning to their restored class-rooms. In January of this year they entered into full occupation of the new building.

The library is no longer within the main building; it has been constructed apart, on the east side of the college lawn, and every modern expedient has been employed to make it proof against future similar destruction. It is being carried out on the scale to receive 120,000 volumes, and the design has been adopted with the view of permitting its extension, when, in future time, the wealth of the library will fortunately exact it.

Great sorrow throughout the province was felt at this national loss, and immediate steps were taken to make it good. Provincial and private subscriptions flowed into the exchequer. In the mother country, the sympathy took the form of reconstructing the library. A public committee was formed, of which Lord Lorne was elected chairman, and great efforts were made to obtain contributions ; pre-eminent among the donors were the Queen, and Emperor of Germany.

The governments of Europe and that of the United States generously aided in every way that was possible. The Australian provinces practically shewed their sympathy ; while the universities of the mother country and of the continent added valuable contributions. In many cases, renowned men of letters sent their books with their autograph presentation.

The consequence has been that the university and the library are again established. A sigh may now and then be given to the fine old library hall by those who knew it, but there is little fear that there will be weeping when the second temple shall be witnessed in its completeness. The thought will be rather that of congratulation, that the university is so happily entering upon its new life, that the restored building is a positive, existent, material fact, and that the new library "flashes now a phœnix," to increase in extent and usefulness.

I have mentioned the rare classical editions which the university formerly possessed. I am informed that a special fund is being raised to replace as far as possible this admirable collection, including the works on archæology and the noble volumes of the Greek and Latin authors, once the pride of the library. The generation which was personally cognizant of Dr. McCaul's fame as an epigrammatist *facile princeps*, will doubtless regard the intention as a special appeal to aid in this integration. It will also be an intimation received with great satisfaction by those who do not consider education to consist merely of the three R's, "reading, 'riting and 'rithmetic," that the valuable private library of the late doctor has been presented to the university. Those who knew and estimated his sound and refined scholarship must offer their congratulations to the senate on this acquisition. By all accounts, the library building is in so advanced a condition that it may possibly be occupied by the end of October. The number of works at present on the catalogue is about 25,000, consisting of 41,500 volumes.

---

* I am indebted to the kindness of the president, Sir Daniel Wilson, for the information contained in the text. Sir Daniel was good enough to place in my hands revised proofs of a pamphlet which he is about publishing, in acknowledgment of the consideration and sympathy received by the University, in the hour of misfortune.

The library of Queen's University is limited in extent, containing 20,000 volumes. The books are well selected; the accommodation of the building will admit double the number. Last year the additions were noteworthy, being Guizot's "Collection des Mémoires," and Petitot's well-known collection, 131 volumes. It is anticipated that this branch of literature will shortly be increased by Pertz' "Monumenta Historica Germanica," and Muratori's collection of Italian annals : with these additions the sources of information as of mediæval history will be as complete as we may look for in ordinary circumstances.

The University has of late so enlarged its operations in the material effort of adding new buildings, and of appointing new professors to meet the increased number of students, that the annual expenditure for the library is somewhat cramped. The fact is well known among the old graduates, and the feeling is very strong that some effort should be made to establish a library fund. The amount of $50,000 has been named as a desirable endowment. It would furnish nearly $3,000 a year, and this amount judiciously spent on books, would, in half a century, effect great results. The late Mr. Robert Sutherland, of Walkerton, a graduate of the University, recently left the library his collection of law books, and Mr. Alexander Morris his collection of works on Canadian history. Those whose circumstances admit of substantially aiding the University in this respect, whether graduates whose early life was passed within its precincts, or men, whose connection with it is that of sympathy and appreciation, should bear in mind, how well applied any beneficence in this direction on their part will be.

It is only within the last ten years that systematic efforts

have been made to widen the scope of the library of
Trinity College. Until that date it had been limited chiefly
to the standard works of the Church of England and of
patristic literature, with several volumes of well-known non-
episcopal writers. The present provost introduced the
system of an annual appropriation, which is expended
generally on history and the other branches of literature.
Theological works, however, continue to obtain the preference. Classics form one of the most striking features in
the library, consisting of 1,500 volumes, among which is
Valpy's edition of the Delphin classics [1819–1830]. The
supporters of Trinity College cannot more wisely aid the
institution than by augmenting the library.

Trinity College dates from the 17th of March, 1851, when
the first sod was turned by Bishop Strachan. On the
secularization of the National University of King's College,
it was resolved to establish a Theological University for the
clergy of the Church of England, which at the same time
would admit lay students. It obtained a royal charter,
dated the 16th of July, 1853. Its endowment was the result
of subscriptions obtained in the mother country by Bishop
Strachan, and the money collected in Canada. The design
of Mr. Kivas Tully having been accepted, the corner stone
was laid by Bishop Strachan on the 30th of April, 1851, and
the first service was performed in the college chapel on the
15th of January, 1852, when the main building was occupied
for the purposes of the college.*

* On this occasion Bishop Strachan gave the following account
of the success of his mission in England. Speaking of his
application to obtain the means of endowment, he said:—" In
this the two great Church Societies and the University of Oxford
took the lead. The Society for the Propagation of the Gospel in
Foreign Parts voted two thousand pounds, payable by instalments

The above brief narrative will shew the difficulties with which the institution has had to contend, and it furnishes an explanation, if the library is in some respects not perfectly equipped.

The Legislative Library in Toronto has never been the object of great favour on the part of the members of the house, consequently, it has remained within a somewhat narrow limit. It contains possibly some 8,000 works, set forth in the catalogue; books of value generally well selected. It makes no pretence to being more than a library of reference, and no specialty has been developed. Last year a new catalogue was issued, by which the character of the books can be judged. It shews the weakness of the library in many respects, and it may probably have the good effect of inducing members of the legislatures to put to themselves the pertinent question, if the parliamentary library of rich and prosperous Ontario should be without any of the classical authors, or contain no books on its shelves in any other language but that of English; and whether in the interest of the members themselves, the library ought, or ought not to be kept up to the horizon of modern thought in sociology,

---

of four hundred pounds per annum, and a donation of seven acres and a half of land within the precincts of the City of Toronto worth at least as much more. The Society for Promoting Christian Knowledge granted three thousand, and the University of Oxford five hundred pounds. The subscriptions from individuals throughout England exceed four thousand pounds, in sums of tens, twenties and fifties, up to £104, from Liverpool. One generous benefactor deserves particular notice, Charles Hampden Turner, Esquire, F.R.S., Rook's Nest Park, Surrey, who has given us the princely gift of five hundred pounds."

history and political philosophy. This view cannot have failed to present itself to several members of a house containing many educated men. The Legislature of Ontario is not under the conditions of a university, struggling to increase its professors, to extend its buildings, and yearly to obtain costly works of reference, not simply in English, but in the European continental languages. There is no proper expenditure of this character which the popular vote of Ontario will not fully justify. It would in my judgment be an acceptable policy to place the parliamentary library at the standard which the dignity of the province suggests. A few years' liberal appropriation would attain the happiest result. The very atmosphere of a well supplied library has an elevating effect on the minds of those who breathe it. One of its teachings to any man of sense is to suggest the reflection, how much is to be read and pondered over, before the higher duties of life can be, with the best intentions, wisely and efficiently performed.

The Public Library of Toronto is deserving of mention from the energy displayed in its establishment, and the success which has attended its operation. Its existence was legalized by the Free-Library By-Law voted on the 1st of January, 1883.* The building in Church Street formerly used as the Mechanics' Institute was obtained, and enlarged so as to afford space for 150,000 volumes. The library was formally opened on the 6th of March, 1884, by the Lieutenant-Governor, Hon. John Beverley Robinson. Branch libraries were early established. There are now four

* The Free Libraries Act was passed by the Ontario Legislature in March, 1882.

such branches, where books can be obtained, viz., North, at Saint Paul's Hall; East, at Bolton Avenue; West, at Dundas Street; and at Saint Andrew's market. The present collection consists of 75,000 volumes, to which yearly additions are made: divided, as a circulating library of 42,000; and 33,000 as a reference library. The number of readers for last year was 31,500; 22,000 of whom obtained books from the central library. The total issue of books this year is estimated at half a million. The institution is unusually rich in books bearing upon the history of the continent, especially in all that relates to Canada, to which branch of study special attention is given.*

It is also in possession of complete sets of the Societies' publications, such as the Maitland Club, the Camden, the Shakespeare, etc., etc. Several valuable MSS. have been collected, especially the papers of Sir David W. Smyth, the first surveyor-general of Upper Canada from 1794 to 1804. They consist of twenty-four MS. volumes, and contain copies of his reports, with the letters addressed to him by Governor Simcoe and the leading men of that date. They include the original applications for land grants from the U.E. Loyalists; the original plans of towns and villages, minutes of the commissioners, with several hundred private letters. So valuable is this collection that it is a matter of wonder that it escaped the unceasing vigilance of the British Museum librarians.

Our own government is unfortunately indifferent regarding such acquisitions, for any surprise to be expressed that it passed unnoticed in Ottawa. With proper representation the House of Commons is most liberal in such votes. The

---

* On this matter I can speak with confidence. Through the considerate kindness of the librarian, Mr. Bain, I have obtained access to books which I could find nowhere else.

128

Minister has only to ask to obtain a fair grant for any legitimate purpose. Let us hope that the teaching of this event will not be lost. We may, however, feel grateful that these valuable papers are a permanent acquisition of the country. Under the admirable management of the Toronto Library they are accessible to the fullest extent. Such documents, however, are national, and should be possessed by the Archive branch, and included in its system. On such special occasions when original papers bearing upon the history of the country are offered for sale, the government should rise to the height of the occasion, and obtain all valuable documents of the class, and not be afraid to pay for them what is fair and reasonable. For where there is any haggling with regard to the money, those who act with liberality gain possession of the prize, and the papers are lost by those who should possess them.

The existence of the present library in Toronto is one of the highest honours which the city possesses; the number of readers shows the good use to which it is put. The issue of books increases at the rate of ten per cent annually, and, what is a healthy symptom, the demand of mere works of fiction "steadily decreases." The library authorities have been at some pains systematically to determine the fact. I owe it to their industry * to be able to state that in 1888 the proportion of works of fiction issued for home reading amounted to 66.5 of the whole: in 1891, it was reduced to 53.1 per cent. Taking into consideration the miscellaneous character of the class of readers gathered from the entire population of the city, this proportion may be considered in every way encouraging. The whole hope of the future of Canada lies in the sound, sober sense of the community, by

* [Report 1891.]

which opinion is influenced. It is by reading and thought that men of this character are moulded. By slow degrees only the class can be increased ; but when the beginning is once made, the teaching penetrates into strata, where its influence with many is unlooked for. We have passed the first stage in Toronto, and there is ground for hope that the future will bring forth fair fruit.

With regard to the library itself, it has already gained a deservedly high reputation. In half a century it will be one of the foremost institutions of the continent. Its management is unimpeachable.

In 1885, the library received from alderman John Hallam the handsome gift of two thousand volumes, of which a special catalogue has been published.*

The library of the Law Society of Ontario is to be found in Osgoode Hall, the seat of the principal law courts and chambers of the judges. The society was incorporated in 1822 : the present building completed in 1860. The library is established in a well proportioned chamber, of much

---

* I am indebted to Senator Almon for the perusal of a *brochure* to which I can, with propriety, allude in these pages. "The Charter and By-laws of the New York Society Library with a catalogue of the books belonging to the said library. New York. Printed by H. Gaine, Printer, Bookseller and Stationer, at the Bible and Crown in Hanover Square, 1773."

The Society was established by Royal Charter dated the 9th of November, 1772, under the last royal governor William Tryon. The catalogue records 477 works, all of them English. Some translations of the classics and of French standard works are in the list, but no work in those languages. This *brochure* is one of the many rare books collected by Dr. Almon in connection with the history of the continent, of which he has been a diligent student.

I

architectural pretension ; from the airiness of the situation and the subdued re-echo of the street noise, owing to the distance from it, the place is well adapted for study and literary examination.

As can be well imagined, the principal feature is, that it is a law library ; it contains about 25,000 volumes, and is fairly complete in English, Canadian, and United States statutes, treatises, legal reports, and modern periodicals ; it may, indeed, claim to include the reports of every state and territory of the United States. There has been the continuous effort to possess every work in our language of practical benefit to the profession, all new editions of importance being obtained on their appearance. The statutes of England, from the great charter to modern times, are unusually complete.

The political literature is represented by the parliamentary journals and Hansards of the mother country, and of the several provinces, with those of the dominion. There are excellent editions of the Greek and Latin classics, with from 2,000 to 3,000 volumes of general historical literature, reference dictionaries, biographies, *et id genus*. What is not a common acquisition is a complete series of the *Times* from 1805 to 1870. One feels a shade of regret that it has not been continued ; the possession of so rare a series suggests that it would be wise to resume and complete the collection.

Many curious law books are on the shelves for reference. The original folio editions of the old English reports, dating back to the black letter of the seventeenth century ; the Statutes of the Realm, issued by the Record Commissioners, 1235–1704, twelve folio volumes [1810–1828] ; the folio volumes of "Campbell's MS. Reports," containing the cases decided by the judges of the King's Bench [1823–1827] the first recorded decisions of the province ; what are known as

"Taylor's printed reports;" with all modern reports. There is likewise a presentation copy of the Queen's printed works with her Majesty's autograph.

The annual increase is 1,200 volumes, the cost of maintenance falling upon the Law Society of Ontario.

There is much consideration shewn in the regulations regarding the books; indeed, the management leaves little to be desired. The library is open from 9 to 5, except in vacation, when the hours are from 10 to 3; every week-day, admission can be obtained from 7.30 to 10 p.m., when any person of respectability is admitted with the privilege of study.

There are three well executed life-size portraits by the late Mr. Berthon on the walls: viz., of the late Chancellor Blake, and the two late Chief-Justices, Sir John Beverley Robinson and Sir James B. Macaulay.*

I am generally indebted to the courtesy of the present librarian, Mr. W. Geo. Eakins, for being able to give the above information.

I have endeavoured in these pages to place on record much which, I humbly conceive, should not be allowed to pass out of notice, and which I trust will not be without its usefulness. I do not pretend that the enumeration in any one class is perfect; but I may say, that the facts open to investigation have been diligently examined. No unimportant stage in any generalization is attained, when it can be established that error exists, for it is the first step towards its rectification. The volume, at least, is an attempt to

* I have been informed that some of the friends of the late Mr. Hillyard Cameron have considered the advisability of obtaining a well executed portrait of this distinguished jurist and amiable man.

place in accessible form all that is known of the subject of which it treats; so that the student may have a starting-point in his research, and the collector be aided in his attempt to bring together the volumes which bear upon the early history of the Dominion.

In the degree that the political literature of a country is studied, and its teaching wisely applied, the institutions under which men live become more adapted to human wants. Every one, however limited his education, desires a pure system of law and justice, administered by capable and honourable men. Likewise, as a theory, every individual recognizes the necessity of our representative institutions being worked out with integrity and wisdom. The attainment of this result lies in the public virtue and patriotism of constituencies. So long as corruption is rampant in the ranks of voters, they will be represented by men who regard cunning as ability, trick as policy, impudence of assertion as force of argument. We have a painful experience of what majorities can, and do vote. Men, honourable in their private relations, justify in parliament a line of conduct repugnant to the national conscience, which, in their home intercourse between man and man, they would scout as basely dishonourable. Party spirit has degenerated into the doctrine that everything is fair in politics, the one duty being to accept the policy which the exigencies of a ministry may determine, whatever the meanness of spirit by which it is characterized. Some dozen men of ability and force of character in the house of commons, with the independence of thought, not to be dragged down to sustain what is wrong and despicable because the caucus so determined, "the deformity of fraud ill-disguised," would go far to purify our political condition, and redeem it from the cancer which is destroying all that is honourable and good in public life. It is in this direction we have to look for better days. The presence of a few such men in parliament who will ably and fairly discuss a measure proposed, and conscientiously sustain or reject it, would, in no long time, work wonders, for it would help to form and educate public opinion. It is to bring into prominence such men that the effort should be continuous to displace the unscrupulous partizan, and the uneducated charlatan.

Constituencies uninfluenced by corruption cannot fail to be represented in each case by an honourable man, not by the apostle of dishonest expediency. The Horatian maxim, "*Fortes creantur fortibus et bonis,*" is as politically true of a community as when Horace asked that the youth of Rome should by strict discipline be taught virtue and patriotism.*

It would be a fortunate day for Canada if we could banish to limbo, as Milton describes it, the paradise of fools, the political leader, successful only by his subterfuge and purchased support: the individual, profuse in his professions, unscrupulous in his preservation of power, poltroon-like secretly striking all whose opposition he dreads, retaining at his bidding an expectant crowd ready by servile meanness to gain advancement. We only owe it to constituencies, when this repellent personage comes into prominence. In order to avoid this national misfortune, the first condition is, that the voter be guided to a proper sense of his elective duty; and

---

* Doctrina sed vim promovet insitam,
  Recteque cultus pectora roborant;
  Utcumque defecere mores,
  Indecorant bene nata culpae.

ODES, iv., 4.

---

Honest men are produced by the honest and good.

But good teaching improves the natural force of character, and the culture of what is right gives strength to the heart; wherever morality is wanting vice degrades endowments in themselves excellent.

134

before we succeed in inculcating a purer political philosophy, we must break some of the images of clay which have been set up for our worship. We must also chase away the false theories of ability too generally accepted, and cease to regard as proper for imitation, that which is inherently vicious. We must begin to teach, in the impressionable years of youth, the penalty inflicted on the Commonwealth by the abandonment of good principles. If the lessons of history have any worth, they shew, that however great a temporary success may be, there is a hereafter, which places at its right estimate every departure from honesty, and that the power achieved by fraud, has no permanency of place for good in the nation's memory.

The records of the past are worthy of continued study, from the teaching which they give to shape the present, by shewing that in the long race of life, the well-being of a community lies in the observance of what is right. As with individuals it is with masses of men. Passionate wrong, and injustice, work back their effect on those who commit them. Success foully gained, retains the taint of the corruption whence it is generated. As history appeals to us, it extends the warning to constituencies, that if they and their children's children are to be prosperous and happy, they must act in accordance with the responsibilities which accompany the privileges they possess; that personally in each individual case they sustain the principles by which nations prosper and become great, and that failure in the performance of this duty brings disaster and ruin. This is the truth we learn from the earliest record of traditional history, and it furnishes one of the many urgent reasons, why its sources should be earnestly sought out, and their truth established.

THE END.

## ADDENDUM.

The following publication has to be included in the early printed books of Ontario, described pp. 27–42 :

"The | Constitution | of the | Bible | and Common Prayer Book | Society | of Upper Canada | established in the town of York | on the 3rd day of December 1816 | with an address | and a list of the | subscribers and contributors | York | Printed by R. C. Horne 1816." 16pp.

# INDEX.